Midlife Motherhood

St. Martin's Griffin

NEW YORK

Midlife Motherhood

A WOMAN-TO-WOMAN GUIDE TO
PREGNANCY AND PARENTING

Jann Blackstone-Ford, M.A.

www.stmartins.com

Grateful acknowledgment is made for permission to reprint an excerpt from "The Road Not Taken" from *The Poetry of Robert Frost,* edited by Edward Connery Lathem. Copyright 1916, © 1969 by Henry Holt and Company, copyright 1944 by Robert Frost. Reprinted by permission of Henry Holt and Company, LLC

Book design by Gretchen Achilles

Library of Congress Cataloging-in-Publication Data

Blackstone-Ford, Jann.
    Midlife motherhood : a woman-to-woman guide to pregnancy and parenting / by Jann Blackstone-Ford.
       p. cm.
    ISBN 0-312-28131-5
    1. Pregnancy in middle age—Popular works. 2. Childbirth in middle age—Popular works. 3. Middle-aged mothers—Popular works. I. Title.
    RG556.6 .B53 2002
    618.2—dc21   2002003649

FIRST EDITION: NOVEMBER 2002

10 9 8 7 6 5 4 3 2 1

To my little Harleigh,
who hated how long it took me to write this book
but loved that it was all about her.
You are my inspiration.

Author's Note

With a few exceptions, the names and identifying characteristics of the people who provided me with their experiences and insights for publication in this book have been changed. In some instances, people requested that their real names be used.

This book is for informational purposes and is not intended to take the place of medical advice from a trained professional. The fact that an organization or Web site is listed in this book as a potential source of information does not mean that the author or publisher endorses any of the information it may provide or recommendations it may make. Further, readers should be advised that Web sites offered as sources for information may have changed since this was written.

Contents

Acknowledgments

There are some people I must thank and without whose help I could not have written this book. First, to my family for your patience and understanding while I wrote. I love you all very much. My thanks to all the women of both the over40mommies Internet group and the midlifemother Internet group who so unselfishly confided their personal thoughts and feelings. My thanks to the women in the Midlife Motherhood support group for their devotion and wisdom, and to all those who contributed stories via the Midlife Motherhood Web site, *www.midlifemother.com.* My thanks to Darcie Johnston for her support and suggestions, and to Jeannette Brandt for her inspiration. My thanks to my sister for listening to me when I had writer's block and for her undying support of anything I do. My thanks to Luba Djurdjinovic, director of the Ferre Institute, for her contribution on infertility, and to Jane Honnikman, of Postpartum Support International, for her help in preparing the section on postpartum depression. Many thanks to Ginny Porter for her time and effort in preparing the "I Don't Have Time, I'm a Mother Workout," and to my friend Tina for so precisely modeling each exercise. I would also like to thank Dr. William Gilbert of UC Davis Medical Center for answering my questions and supplying answers in lay terms so that even I could understand, and to everyone at ParentSoup and iVillage.com for their support of this project. Many thanks to my agent, Djana Pearson Morris, for keeping me on the straight and narrow, and last, but certainly not least, to my editor, Heather Jackson, and her assistant, Lindy Settevendemie, for their support and patience while preparing this manuscript.

Introduction

As I write this my mother-in-law is finally asleep. She lies in a bed next to my computer, peaceful at last, while my daughter bounces her basketball downstairs in the entryway. I cringe when I hear the noise. "Shhhh!" I think. "Don't wake up Grandma." She knows she's not supposed to do that, bounce that ball in the house. It cracks the grout in the tile, but she's doing it to catch my attention. "Come on, Mom!" she shouts. "Let's go shoot some hoops!"

"Help me up and hand me my cane," I think. That was something my father used to say in jest when I as a young girl wanted him to play with me. All of a sudden I get it, and as I stand up from the computer, weary from being spread too thin, I smile at my awakened mother-in-law. "I'll be back in a sec, Mom. Will you be OK?" She smiles back sleepily and I head across the street with my daughter for those hoops.

As we walk, my daughter's hand in mine, small bits of my life flash before my eyes. I've known that woman upstairs in the bed for over thirty years. She gave me my first job at sixteen, and little did I know when she was teaching me to give change that I would be caring for her when she was older. I married her son almost twenty years later, after a fluke reintroduction following my divorce. Her son and I had gone to high school together and after facing some of life's trials—divorce and the death of a parent, his smile was strangely comforting. Marrying him was the second smartest thing I ever did.

The first smartest thing was to have this child whose hand is pulling me across the street. I met opposition, from friends, from family, from society, but for me it was the right thing to do. "Why are you smiling, Mommy?" my daughter asked. I chuckled to myself. "I was just remembering, honey. Remembering about having you."

We had so many close calls that when I finally did become pregnant I knew my husband wouldn't believe me, so I made the doctor confirm it in a letter. My hand trembled a little as I handed him the note. He took it from me with a kind of "what-is-this" look on his face.

I had taken a home pregnancy test the day before, my tenth in three years. This time I had chosen the one that showed a plus sign when you were pregnant and a minus sign when you were not. They were the least expensive. Sometimes you can even buy two in a box, and I anticipated having to use the additional one next month. "Nope, honey," my husband said when he had looked at the results. "That's only a half a plus. It's not a full plus. Don't get your hopes up."

So, it was no wonder that when I presented him with a note from the doctor he was still skeptical. "Yes, Mr. Ford, your wife is four weeks pregnant." He did not look up. He just kept reading the words over and over again.

I was almost forty years old and somewhere along the way I had acquired a condition that made pregnancy merely a question to ponder. "Just one more operation should do the trick," our specialist told us. Then there was the problem of my husband's vasectomy. "You do realize," my doctor told me, "that if you get pregnant it will be a miracle." But destiny was on our side, even if there was only half a plus.

"Okay," my husband said finally looking up from the handwritten note, "but we're still naming it Harley, even if it's a girl." Harleigh Marie Ford was born in early spring and now, at nine, she was holding my hand as we headed for the court.

According to a National Vital Statistics Report, "The only age groups for which birth rates have consistently increased are women aged thirty years and over." Although the teenage birth rate continues to drop, the increase in the number of babies born to women over thirty-five is staggering.

But *I* was feeling out of sync. Although I seemed to fit into the physical demographic of women having babies at midlife, with it came unexpected changes in my outlook for which I was unprepared. After twenty years in the workforce, climbing—and I do mean c-l-i-m-b-i-n-g—up the corporate ladder, I simply had no desire to keep on keepin' on. I knew I could do it. I had been promoted to "the director," but I also knew that time slips through your fingers and my children would be grown in the blink of an eye. I had been there, and done that. I was embarrassed to say that a successful career *outside the home* just wasn't important to me anymore, and I secretly felt as if I was letting down my sisters of the women's movement—the ones that had sacrificed in the '60s and '70s, the ones I stood next to while fighting for equality in the workplace. There was safety in those numbers. I was part of a movement. But now I wanted to stay home and be with my baby. Becoming a mother once again, but this time at midlife, had completely changed my priorities!

I knew I wasn't the only one going through a sort of reverse identity crisis. There had to be more of us out there, but where to find them? There was no literature, no role models. I felt I was forging ahead in uncharted waters. This was a strange feeling for a woman who prided herself in being a take-the-bull-by-the-horns sort of gal. I was feeling insecure for the first time in a very long time, and it was about something so natural, my place as a mother. I needed validation in my choices, to find other women who shared my midlife mother fears and concerns, all while experiencing the first of many hot flashes, I might add. They say God only gives you what you can handle. I decided that God, indeed, has a sense of humor.

That's when I realized there was a need for a book, a book that celebrated midlife motherhood, that warned you of the stumbling blocks and held your hand as you jumped. Sisterhood in book form! And I started reaching out to other midlife mothers for their contributions. I began by building a Web site, *www.midlifemother.com,* which served as a meeting place for women who wanted to contribute to the project. I began to set up meetings, get E-mails and phone calls. This evolved into an e-group, an Internet community where midlife mothers from all over the world came to share their hopes and dreams. From their candid confessions I realized that everyone was the same. We all had the same worries throughout our pregnancies. We all had the same problems with readjustment. We all were facing menopause, toddlers, and elder care all at the same time. Many of us were divorced, remarried to younger men, and trying to blend families while adding to them. Once again, I had found safety in numbers.

Perhaps you will recognize yourself somewhere in the stories of these mothers who so honestly confided in me. Their stories are all true, although some did ask me to change their names. This book, *Midlife Motherhood*, was written to validate your decision to go forward. It acknowledges the pitfalls, but more important honors the celebration. My thanks to you all. It's an honor to be in the club.

ONE

The Road Less Traveled

Two roads diverged in a wood, and I—
I took the one less traveled by,
And that has made all the difference.

—ROBERT FROST

"In a word, I truly feel AGELESS! Seriously, as I approached forty, I had some trouble with admitting my age. It all changed as I became pregnant. I reveled in the fact that this body could make and sustain life and feed my newborn. I felt so sexy and alive. This last summer I went NUTS! Hip huggers and sports bras, glitter belly gel and a fake belly ring! People were shocked and shaken! I no longer fear an empty nest, or what I will do in my dotage. It has given me a new lease on life, and all my friends say that I look/feel rejuvenated—I attribute it all to a sense of purpose, great happiness, and, of course, lots of sex with a younger man . . ."

—DIANE ALBRIGHT, MIDLIFE MOTHER EXTRAORDINAIRE

Who Are We?

Unlike women of past generations who married young and built their lives with their children in tow, we mothers at midlife have made different choices. We have chosen to explore our personal capabilities first, believing that the added wisdom we gained would make us better parents in the future. We are bold, strong, resilient women. We have pasts, faced ups and downs, and that is what has brought us to this point ready to take on yet another challenge—motherhood at midlife.

There are definite reasons why we have come to this place at this time in our lives. First, women are now more healthy than ever before and the medical complications of having a child at midlife are not the grave concerns they once were. In recent years the projected life span of both parents has increased and the likelihood of dying and leaving a young child alone is less probable.

Second, over the last twenty years many women opted for jobs in their early twenties and thirties and have waited until they were well established in their careers before starting a family. Now in approaching forty, the ticking biological clock is not only an emotional desire to have children but a very real physical one. It is not uncommon for women in their forties to experience the first signs of menopause, thereby eliminating their ability to ever have children without the aid of science. If we are going to have children, *now* is the time.

Third, relaxed social mores allow single women and same-sex partners more options to have families.

Fourth, and perhaps the most significant reason why women are having children at midlife, is the rate of divorce in our country. The Bureau of Vital Statistics tells us since 1994, each year, half of all first marriages end in divorce and that the average age of a woman going through a divorce in the United States is thirty-three. The same source also points to the fact that most people wait approximately five years to remarry. Allow a person a couple of years to become readjusted in marriage and you now have a forty-year-old woman contemplating starting a family.

I have to admit, it's a little disconcerting to learn that you fit perfectly into a statistical demographic. Statistics are always about other people. But here I am, one of the many women who became a midlife mother because of a divorce. Although I had a daughter at twenty-nine and tried to get it together in the marriage department, life's bumps slowed me down. By the time my divorce was final, I remarried, and overcame an infertility problem that I didn't know I had, I was thirty-nine years old, and I had unknowingly signed on for two of the biggest undertakings of my life at the same time—becoming both a new mother *and* a stepmother at the same time. Since so many of us are taking on this awesome responsibility, I will devote more time to this subject later. For now, let's meet some fellow midlife moms who also unknowingly fit perfectly into that midlife mother demographic. You will probably see someone you know, if not yourself, in the words of these women.

Meet the Parents

THE CAREER WOMAN

Doris Shaw's story is typical of career women who choose to have a child at midlife. "Before I became pregnant I devoted every waking moment to my career," she says. "After I was promoted it took me a year to get my new sales territory into shape, but I loved my job so I didn't mind. Having a child was always part of my overall game plan, but I woke up one day and I was forty. The deciding factor was when I changed gynecologists and the nurse, not familiar with my medical history, asked if I was still having periods. 'What?' I was astonished by the question. I went home that night and announced to my husband that it was time. That biological clock was ticking very loudly."

Doris explained how having her son has impacted her life. "You really can't compare having a career to having a family. Three years ago my life was business lunches, client trips, and sales meetings. Just being at home with Chase for three months on maternity leave made me realize I couldn't continue the way I had been. I envy women who can juggle it all. I can't. I suppose it would have been different if I *had* to work, but I don't. My husband's law practice does just fine and I felt guilty leaving Chase with a baby-sitter when it wasn't necessary. I know a lot of woman would disagree with me, and sometimes I feel embarrassed to say I no longer work outside of the home. That's my own insecurity I'm working through.

"I never knew how much my identity was wrapped up in what I did for a living until I decided to quit my job. My husband and I were at a party with some new people we had never met before. One of the wives, perhaps ten years younger than I, asked what I did for a living, and I said, 'Right now? I'm a mommy.' It seemed like the room went quiet. I saw myself ten years ago in her eyes and I suspected what she thought of me. They, especially the women, thought I was lazy. I should have been able to both work and raise a child. Ten years ago I still had to prove something to someone. Most of all, myself. But, you know, I've done all that. Now, I've moved on to the next stage of my life, and I'm very happy where I am right this minute."

DIVORCE AND REMARRIAGE

Kathy Singer is a real estate broker in the San Francisco Bay Area. Because of soaring housing prices, she has done extremely well over the last ten years. She looks exactly like what you would think a high-end real estate broker would look like. Perfect skin from lots of facials, lots of winter white, including her hair, and gold jewelry. I have been talking to her for the last fifteen minutes and she has not talked about anything but the housing market. Having children was not in her game plan.

"I was married the first time to a man who didn't want children," she says. "I didn't think I wanted them either. I was pregnant once, but we decided on abortion, and I never got pregnant again. We divorced after ten years and I spent ten more years building my business.

"I guess I was looking for family and didn't even know it. I met John because his company offered him a promotion and relocation, and he took it. My office handled the relocation. John's first wife had died and left him alone with a ten-year-old daughter, Trisha. He wanted to start over, so he moved to the Bay Area. I fell in love with them immediately and wanted to adopt Trisha, but she had strong recollections of her biological mother and secretly compared us all the time. Because of this, she kept me at arm's length and our period of adjustment was rocky." Kathy closed her eyes and mock shivered. "Don't want to go through that again.

"One day when Trisha and I were particularly at odds I sat down with her and we had a very frank talk. I told her that I knew that she would always have a special place in her heart for her mother and that I wanted to help her keep that place special just for her feelings and memories of the woman she missed so much. I asked her if she thought that her mother would want her to be angry and sad. She answered no, thank goodness. What would I have done if she answered me differently? Then I asked her if she could look on it as if I was simply helping her mommy. Her mother couldn't stay on this earth to take care of her, and it was my job to help from now on. I explained I didn't want to take her mommy's place, it was just now my responsibility to help keep her safe, and that I, too, loved her very much.

"Where I found those words, I don't know. It was like someone was sitting next to me, whispering in my ear. *Now say this*, the voice would say, and I just said the words. Not long after our talk my daughter introduced me as her mother for the first time. I can't begin to describe the feeling."

"I'm not sure when family became so important to me. This was not my intent. I had no plans to be this maternal. In fact, I didn't think it was my nature, but then I got involved with this family, and for the first time in my life, I felt needed. At work, I know I'm needed, but it's not the same. At home, I make a difference in someone's life, and they in mine. When you don't have a family is when you realize the importance of having one. And, for what its worth, after forty years, I finally have mine."

And, at forty-three, Kathy Singer added to her family—a healthy little girl named Jolie.

THE SINGLE MOTHER

In years past the social stigma of having a child outside of marriage prevented single women from openly raising children outside of wedlock. That same social stigma also prevented single women from considering adoption as a possibility. Although there are some that still view single women having children as "wrong," it is not the taboo it once was. Single midlife moms are everywhere, and they have their own personal midlife mom issues and concerns.

Heather is a single woman who, at forty-three, lives with her parents because of pre-existing medical conditions. Heather is in the process of *trying* to conceive her first child—alone. "I was shocked at my parents' reaction when I told them that I wanted to do this. They were extremely supportive and they are excited and hopeful for a happy healthy pregnancy. They are, of course, worried about my health. Other than my age, I have some pre-existing conditions that could complicate things. I live with my parents and they will be helping me raise my child. My mother is exceptional, so I will be looking to her for advice.

Heather is not looking to marry someone in order to have a child. "I'm forty-three with no prospects. And, I want a child. What else is there to do?"

Cyndi had a problem. As a registered nurse and completely dedicated to her career, there was no time to find "Mr. Right," and as time went on it just wasn't that important.

"I simply had no time for relationships, so if I wanted to be a mother, single motherhood was my only option. I stopped the pill at age thirty-five. Then came the dreaded infertility chase—for eleven years."

Cyndi was single. "If I did have an occasional lover, we always used a condom for fear of STDs. How the heck was I supposed to get pregnant?" She laughed. "This was all before it was chic to be pregnant and single. Society can be very harsh on liberal thinking."

Cyndi kept her eyes and ears open and soon heard about an organization called Single Mothers By Choice, out of New York. "I immediately inquired and started receiving their newsletter. Then I was watching TV one day and I stumbled on a show about women who chose to be single mothers. I took that to be a sign. I made my decision to try artificial insemination right then and there.

"My mother did not speak to me for days after I told her the news. Her generation, and my upbringing, didn't accept children out of wedlock. I basically told her that I was not seventeen and knocked up, that I was a white-collar professional, a homeowner, and that I was making a well-thought-out, conscious choice. She did come around and soon became my biggest fan. This was her first chance to be a grandmother and one day she secretly confessed that her friends' grandbaby brag books made her green with envy."

Cyndi started artificial insemination (AI) at thirty-nine with purchased sperm from a donor bank and began an eight-year roller coaster ride toward motherhood. She did not get pregnant after five attempts and one full year. Then came the never-ending diagnostic testing to find the cause. After two laparoscopic procedures, a hystosalpinogram, numerous blood tests, fertility drugs, fresh sperm, frozen sperm, intercourse, more AI attempts and then Intrauterine Insemination (II), there was still no pregnancy. She was told it was time to see an infertility specialist. More blood tests, more fertility drugs. Six years of IVF and more unsuccessful surgeries and she was finally told that her eggs were too old. So she purchased young donor eggs. "I finally got to the point where my heart, body, and soul could no longer endure this madness. When do you stop?" Cyndi asked. "I had gained sixty pounds, and spent over $250,000. I lost time and wages at work and almost my mind. My medical insurance did not cover any of these expenses. The stress and disappointment along with occasional hope created a tremendous amount of emotional turmoil."

Finally, after feeling there was no way she could carry a child to term, she settled on the "adoption option."

"This also was a long, tedious, and expensive journey," Cyndi explained. "But after four years and five potential birth mothers, I have finally become a mother! I am a bona fide midlife mother and lovin' every minute of it. I will receive my AARP card this year, a couple months before my son turns three."

SAME-SEX PARENTS

Today's more relaxed attitude toward a gay lifestyle has given couples like Tory and Sheila, life partners from Southern California, more options than in the past. I have known Tory for years. Before the writing of Midlife Motherhood we had never ventured outside the lines of casual conversation, but now I had an opportunity to ask some very poignant questions about which I had always been curious.

Tory and Sheila are very accomplished women. Both well into their late thirties, Sheila works as a speech pathologist, while Tory is a marriage and family counselor. Even a few years ago their decision to raise a family together would not have been socially accepted, but in today's more tolerant world, it's not that uncommon. With that in mind, five years ago Sheila was artificially inseminated and gave birth to a son. Two years later it was Tory's turn. Her daughter is now three years old.

"We wanted our children to be biologically related," explained Sheila. "It was very important to us to have the family completely connected to one another. Medical science enabled Tory and I to have biological siblings, and we are very happy with our choice." But it wasn't that easy for Tory. "I'm not sure why," said Tory. "Maybe it was all the hormones I took to prepare for the artificial insemination and maintain the pregnancy. Any way you look at it, it was pretty difficult." And then Tory suffered a stroke immediately after she delivered her daughter.

"There I lay, unable to move, unable to hold my baby. It was difficult to breast-feed because I couldn't hold her in the early days. There was a lot of mental confusion from the stroke. Thank goodness my partner, Sheila, was at my side helping me.

Like so many of the midlife moms you will meet in this book, Tory has steered the course and come out a winner. Formerly a physical therapist, she had to change careers because although her stroke did not leave her paralyzed, she was physically weaker and unable to continue in her original profession. "I decided I had to do something different. My mind was strong. I still wanted to help people." Tory went back to school and is now a marriage and family counselor. After overcoming some incredible obstacles, their family is complete.

"I have very strong feelings about what a family is," explained Sheila. "I was adopted, you know. As a matter of fact, my mother and father were at midlife when I came into their lives. My mom was thirty-eight and my father was forty-seven. Because of that, I know that a family is defined by who you live with, who loves you, and who are your advocates on a day-to-day basis. That's your family. The rest is just verbiage. A family isn't defined by your internal biology, but by external actions."

THE UNEXPECTED PREGNANCY

For me, the term unexpected pregnancy has been reserved for either the very young, or the "surprise" baby born to unsuspecting parents after years of marriage. But, after talking to hundreds of midlife moms, I can attest that unexpected pregnancies are alive and well for midlife mothers everywhere. One of my standard questions while preparing my research was, "Was this baby planned?" A surprising number of women answered, "Are you kidding?" When further questioned, some said they thought they were too old to get pregnant, so birth control wasn't used; or they had been told years before that they could never have children. Many were unmarried and the "surprise baby" served as a catalyst for marriage. Any way you look at it, when they took the pregnancy test, the result surprised them.

Madeline is fifty-four years old and on her second life, at least that's the way she explains it. Her thoughts on midlife motherhood are quite amusing, and very true. "We had an 'oops baby'—at least that's what we called him before he was born. At the age of forty-six I woke up pregnant." Madeline laughed. "Well, of course there was more to it than that, but the first thing I said after I took the home pregnancy test was, 'Oops!' We called him 'Oops' all the way through the pregnancy. I have to say, I did consider abortion. I thought maybe my eggs were too old. Aside from the baby's health, we were concerned about my health. Could I sustain a pregnancy and still be healthy after the birth? But, I couldn't abort, even if it meant problems for me. I felt like it was sort of closing the barn door after the cow got out and saying it was the cow's fault. I make all my own decisions. I had a few complications, but nothing lingering. My son is now eight and my husband and I are on our second life and loving it!

And [having a child at midlife] has given my oldest daughter a vocation, believe it or not. She was just finishing up nursing school when we had Justin and she was so fascinated with it she decided to become a midwife. She specializes in births at midlife. I'm so proud of her. And my life is good."

Are You Ready for This One?

Unlike Madeline, who regarded her unplanned pregnancy as a new lease on life, other midlife mothers are shocked by the news and unprepared for the changes ahead: Marni, a working mom from Denver, was happily divorced with two sons well on their way to adulthood when she found out she was pregnant at forty.

"I had been divorced for twelve years, and my sons were fourteen and sixteen years old, when I discovered I was pregnant. Frank and I had met a year before, and he was certainly the most promising of the men I had gone out with over the previous decade, but still I had significant doubts.

"One night I was sitting in the stands watching him coach my son's basketball game, and suddenly it occurred to me that I hadn't had a period for a while. Panicked, I ducked out during halftime and picked up a pregnancy test from the drugstore on the next block. As soon as we got home, I headed straight for the bathroom. The result was immediately obvious. My reaction, in words: Oh shit.

"I didn't tell Frank for more than a week. I needed to sort out my own feelings before they got complicated by his. I knew what he wanted. He wanted to get married. This was a man who should have had six children. He was born to be a dad.

"I did not want to be pregnant. I was single. I had two teenage sons—what was I going to tell them, and what kind of an example was I setting? I was happy with my life the way it was. My boys were almost grown, and I was starting to dream about life changes that I would be able to make soon. I was devastated by this turn of events."

Some midlife mothers must not only adjust to their changing bodies, but also confront the nagging guilt associated with feelings of ambivalence about bringing a child into the world. Their life is set in one direction, and when they find themselves pregnant, the need to change directions only confounds their ambivalent feelings.

"For years after my divorce," explained Marni, "I would ask the Cosmos if I would have any more children, or if I would have a daughter. But those questions had faded, and I had moved on to the next stage of life. Now the Cosmos had answered and I simply wasn't into it. I made an appointment for an abortion—twice—and canceled both times. I wanted time itself to stop and just let me off. I felt paralyzed."

But there was a turn of events for Marni. She did marry Frank and that all-important amniocentesis was scheduled. "I had amniocentesis fairly late, at about fifteen weeks. Now I was completely obsessed with the other side of the spectrum. What if there turned out to be something wrong? I wondered what women do when that happens. I couldn't face having an abortion at six weeks, so how could I possibly do it at sixteen or seventeen or eighteen weeks? And yet, I was already ambivalent about having a normal child . . . the thought of having a child with extraordinary needs was unbearable. I sincerely thank God for not presenting me with that dilemma. The baby turned out to be normal . . . and she was a SHE!"

Finding out the sex of their baby can be the needed wake-up call for mothers who struggle with the news that they are pregnant. It was what Marni needed. "Hearing that the baby was a girl had to be, ironically, one of the happiest days of my life. The joy I felt surprised even me. I wasn't necessarily hoping for one sex or the other, and I think I assumed it would be a boy. I had two boys already. I 'do' boys. I think little boys are adorable and, as teenagers, they're probably easier than girls. But when the technician called out, 'I see a labia!' I was rushed with ecstasy. I was going to get a daughter after all! She was now a person in my eyes and I couldn't wait to meet her."

While it's not uncommon for new mothers like Marni to experience ambivalence when they get the news that they are going to have a baby, others liken having that child to an almost religious experience. They count the days since conception; they note each change in their body with keen anticipation. Eager to discuss their thought processes and why they chose to make this life-changing decision, they start conversations about having children at midlife while standing in line at the post office.

To listen to Lee Anne, a philosophy professor who is now fifty-two, but had her only daughter ten years ago, you would think the skies opened and her little bundle of joy floated down through the clouds with trumpets blaring. The event seemed that profound to her. Her daughter is her soulmate, and you can see it in their eyes when they are together.

"I was on the other side of forty," explained Lee Anne, "when I decided I wanted a child. I had accomplished all I wanted to accomplish and my husband and I were so comfortable in our jobs that we were bored. We are from the generation that believes your career, what you do, is the center of your life's work. It's what you are. Both of our fathers were professors. My husband and I are both professors. We had a very orderly life with lesson plans, planned vacations, and planned parties. There was no spontaneity; everything was anticipated, the product known for what seemed like decades before we got there. Oh, my husband and I were close, I guess. We loved each other, but by that time we had been married for fifteen years and we were settled into an everyday routine where everything was, well, *planned*.

"About a year before my daughter was born, I came down with a very bad case of the flu. My temperature shot up and I tossed and turned in bed, dozing in and out of sleep. I remember having a dream and in this dream I had a child. Having children was the furthest thing from my mind at that point, but nevertheless, I had a child in the dream. I can still see the dream vividly. It was just an image; a fleeting moment, but the child was a little girl. She was around four years old with curly blond hair, and I remember thinking how strange that was because my husband and I both have dark, very straight hair. Anyway, we were walking through a park and this little girl was holding my husband's hand. I was walking beside them. Then, it was as if a camera zoomed in on the little girl's face as she smiled up at me. That was it. That was the dream, but when I woke up, something felt different. I turned to my husband and said, "I want a child. It's time." A year later I had my daughter, and when she was four, the three of us were walking through the park near our home. She smiled up at me and it was the same little face that I saw in the dream. That's why I know this was all meant to be."

How Will This Child Fit into My Life?

I've spoken to quite a few midlife mothers who feel they were destined to have the children that they have. Do we have premonitions? Is it mother's intuition? Do we inherently know this child's place in our lives? On a personal note I knew the exact role I hoped our new baby would play. My husband and I were attempting to blend our family and we knew our new child would be a direct link to each member of the family. This child would not be any single member's "step" or "real sister." She was related to each of us equally and, because of that, a special bond was made with each family member.

We are often asked to clarify which child belongs to which parent, a task that we personally disdain. Each time we are asked about our youngest, all three older children emphatically proclaim, "She's my sister!" which is exactly how my husband and I hoped they would respond. A few weeks after the birth of our youngest child, a new friend decided to explain the interpersonal workings of a stepfamily to my children by attempting to clarify the difference between a step-sister, a real sister, and a half sister. "How can you have half a sister?" asked my six-year-old son. Our new friend did not know how to answer him.

We know that this child serves a purpose in our lives, even though we may not be fully conscious of the reason right at this moment. Could it be to boost your confidence, question your ego, surrender to something greater than yourself, or, as in my case, to unite a family? Whether this child was planned or entered your life through less conventional means, the time you have been graced by this gift is here at middle age, at the middle of your life's journey—not at the beginning where nothing is known for sure, but at the middle, where it appears, you can look both ways before crossing. This child will have the benefit of your past knowledge, plus share in your enthusiasm for the future. He or she will not only open your eyes, but open your heart to what is ahead. Most importantly, whether this child is biological or adopted, you are graced by his or her presence, and this person will become your greatest teacher.

TWO

In Our Own Words—Common Fears and Concerns

"I had a thought just the other day that scared me to death. I am forty-three and just had a baby girl. My goodness, when she's my age, I will be eighty-six! Did I have this child only to burden her with taking care of me when I get older? (Assuming I live that long.) Will she resent me for that? And will she be embarrassed when her dad and I attend all her school functions and are the only parents there with gray hair? I hope not."

—ALISSA MONTGOMERY, A MIDLIFE MOTHER FROM SYDNEY, AUSTRALIA

Before I began to write this book I thought I was alone in my fears and concerns about having a child at midlife. The other midlife moms I had met seemed so self-assured that I thought I was surely the only one who agonized about getting sick, or dying, or having a child with special needs. Surprisingly, I found that all midlife mothers have the same worries. A midlife mother from Australia contributed the opening quote to this chapter, but those same words were echoed by mothers from the U.S., Canada, England, New Zealand, even Sweden.

I always feel more comfortable when I discuss my concerns, either with friends, a therapist, someone who will listen and offer insight as to how to handle that given situation. My goal for this chapter was that in hearing other midlife mothers voice the same concerns that you secretly fear and allowing them to pass on their insights, it would ease your worries and help you to prepare for what is ahead.

Our Number One Concern: Will I Have a Child with Special Needs?

"At first I was worried about the baby. All my life I had heard that if you have a baby when you are older, it may have Down syndrome. When I was a child, children with Down syndrome were called retarded. Doug, down the street, was retarded. To this day I can hear my mother whispering a secret explanation. 'His mother was older, honey.' 'Oh,' I said. Like it was bad to have children when you are older.

"I remember his mother, Ida, knocking on the door, a plate of cookies in one hand, Doug in the other. Ida had two sons—one tall, handsome, but arrogant son named William, who rarely spoke to the little kids, and Doug, who smiled from ear to ear as soon as he walked in the room. Although I could barely understand him when he talked, I knew instinctively by age five that Doug was a gentle soul. It was a huge surprise to find that he was actually two years older than William. So, ironically, at forty-two, when I saw the plus on the pregnancy test, one of the first things that came to mind was Doug. I had not thought of him for almost thirty-five years."

Those are the words of Christina, a tall, willowy woman with slightly salt-and-pepper hair, who was pregnant for the first time at forty-two. It was an unplanned pregnancy: because of a diagnosis long forgotten, Christina was never supposed to have children. She had been married for nineteen years when her periods slowly paused and the fleeting notion that she might be pregnant crossed her mind.

"Because I was told so many years before that I would never have children, I thought I was starting menopause. Isn't that the way it starts? Your periods get lighter until you no longer have them? By the third month my periods were so light, I decided as a lark to take a home pregnancy test. I had never had a reason to do that before and I felt awkward fumbling with the little dropper that comes with the kit. It said to use four drops of urine. Knowing that it was impossible that I was pregnant, I felt silly as I clumsily dropped at least seven drops into the little reservoir. When the test immediately came up positive I thought, Well, I used too many drops. Then I thought of Doug."

MYTH OR MISCONCEPTION

The common belief is that more children with chromosomal abnormalities, such as Down syndrome or spina bifida, are born to women over thirty-five. In actuality, the opposite is true. Since statistics point to an increased possibility of a genetic disorder in a baby born to women after age thirty-five, genetic testing is often suggested to older mothers but not to younger ones. Therefore, statistics point to a higher incident of babies with Down syndrome born to parents *under* thirty-five, not over.

Even with this knowledge, Christina's fears are not unfounded. Her age does suggest an added risk of having a child with chromosomal abnormalities, but let's put her fears into proper perspective. According to the Maternal Risk Chart below, it states the chances of Christina, at age forty-two, having a baby with a risk of any sort of chromosomal damage are approximately one in forty. That sounds huge. My goodness, one in forty! But, translated into a percentage, Christina has *better than a 97 percent chance* of having a healthy baby. It's all how you look at the numbers. Although the risks should be taken seriously, they are not as horrifying as they first appear.

Maternal Risk Chart

MATERNAL AGE (years)	RISK FOR DOWN SYNDROME	TOTAL RISK FOR CHROMOSOMAL DAMAGE
20	1/1,667	1/526
25	1/1,250	1/476
30	1/952	1/385
35	1/378	1/192
40	1/106	1/66
41	1/82	1/53
42	1/63	1/42
43	1/49	1/33
44	1/38	1/26
45	1/30	1/21
46	1/23	1/16
47	1/18	1/13
48	1/14	1/10
49	1/11	1/8

This table originally appeared in *Maternal Fetal Medicine: Practice and Principles*. Creasy and Resnick, eds. W. B. Saunders, Philadelphia, PA. 1994:71. Reproduced with permission of the publisher.

> **Midlife Mom Memo:**
>
> To convert the maternal risk ratio to a percentage of risk, simply convert the ratio to a fraction, and then multiply both the numerator and the denominator by the number necessary to convert the denominator to 100. For example:
>
> STEP 1: 1:25
>
> STEP 2: 1/25
>
> STEP 3: $4 \times 25 = 100$
>
> STEP 4: $4 \times 1 = 4$
>
> STEP 5: 4/100
>
> STEP 6: 4/100 = 4%

GENETIC TESTING: YOUR CHOICE

Alice is a little older than Christina. At forty-four years old, she jokes that she bleaches her hair blond because she can no longer keep up with the gray. Alice spent the first half of her life married to the wrong man and completely dedicated to a career. She divorced and is now married to Jim, an ad executive, ten years her junior. Five years ago Alice had her first child, a few months before her fortieth birthday.

"When I asked my doctor about an amniocentesis, the test that could tell me if the child I was carrying a special needs child, he looked at me very carefully. 'Alice,' he said. 'You are forty-four years old. The possibility of you having a child with Down syndrome is close to 1 in 25. If you believe in abortion, then have the amnio. If you don't believe in abortion, what difference does it make if you have an amnio or not?'" So that night Alice and her husband did some serious talking. In her mind she was still quoting the statistics from when she had her first child at thirty-nine, 1:95. That was under 1 percent and Alice was comfortable with that, but at forty-four the percentage was considerably higher, 1:26, and new fears were added to her climbing list of concerns. "When I got pregnant I had no idea that the chances of having a special needs child increased so rapidly as you grew older," Alice admitted. "Now I was afraid. Were my husband and I prepared for the added responsibilities of a special needs child? But what was the alternative? My God, I couldn't have the amnio until I was sixteen weeks pregnant. The thought of an abortion at sixteen weeks was horrifying to me. Then to wait a week or more for the results? I felt selfish and confused and I hated that I had to make this choice."

An amniocentesis can be performed as early as eleven to fourteen weeks; however, because of a higher chance of miscarriage, the screening is traditionally done when fifteen to twenty weeks' pregnant. Having an amniocentesis is often associated with the pro-choice/pro-life option, but many simply miss the point. Having an amnio does not necessarily mean that you will get an abortion should your child be unhealthy. An amnio can screen for a host of other chromosomal abnormalities besides Down syndrome, and should the baby be affected, there will be time before he or she is born to prepare family members or even secure special facilities if need be.

WHEN YOU FIND OUT THERE IS SOMETHING WRONG

"I did have an amnio and that is when we got his diagnosis," explained Eileen, who was forty-six when her last child was diagnosed with Klinefelter syndrome, a relatively common genetic disorder that occurs in every 500 to 1,000 live male births. "It gave us time to find out about his condition before he was born and prepare my family. Of course I cried at first about it, just because of the unknown, but I am so blessed to have this baby and all my others. Things do work out. He seems to be bright and energetic!! He might encounter some extra bumps on the path of life, but I think he will be fine and have a happy and productive life."

DOWN SYNDROME: THE REALITY

Since the chance of having a child with Down syndrome was the number one fear discussed by mothers having children at midlife, I wanted to introduce someone who had actually faced that hurdle and could pass on her insight. Barbara Curtis is now fifty-three, but started her second family at thirty-five. She has a B.A. in philosophy, graduated magna cum laude, and is a certified Montessori instructor. Barbara is the mother of ten children ages five, six, eight, twelve, thirteen, fifteen, seventeen, eighteen, twenty-six, and thirty-two, including four with Down syndrome—three adopted. She is the grandmother of eight.

"I just kept having children while I was using birth control," she chuckled. "So my husband and I decided we were on a mission from God to have kids." She was only half kidding, but the way she said it reminded me of the movie *The Blues Brothers*. Very matter of fact. *I'm Jake. This is Elwood. We're on a mission from God.* "We had four boys in a row, after I was thirty-five, and then a little girl. When I was pregnant with my son Jonathon, my doctor suggested an amniocentesis, but I declined. My friend had just miscarried twins and it was feared the amnio was the catalyst, so I didn't want to risk it. There was really no point. My husband and I decided long ago that our children were our children, but I don't think my doctor believed me. He really pushed for the amnio. But we figured Jonny was our eighth child and I guess we thought we were off the hook. We had made it this far and all the kids were healthy. We didn't think we would be given more than we could handle. As it is, we were right.

"I like to say my son Jonny has a little extra—a little enthusiasm, a little extra innocence, a little extra charm, and an extra chromosome. The one on the twenty-first pair that puts so much fear in parents-to-be. But it's nothing to fear. My Jonny has taught me so much. It's like walking into another dimension. All of a sudden you realize the things that used to attract you to people, their looks, are nothing. Oh, I know that's something you hear all the time, but Jonny made me live it. He has more joy, more love; he changes a room when he's present. If someone came to me and said, 'With the wave of this magic wand I will take away your son's Down syndrome,' I would have to say no, because Jonny is the purest human being I know."

Barbara was very careful to add that it is important to acknowledge the full spectrum of emotions associated with having a baby born with Down syndrome. "I know there is often grief associated with having a child with Down syndrome. That's only natural. But, personally, I didn't feel grief. I remember holding my child for the first time and actually feeling a sense of relief that something I feared was not as bad as I had imagined. I knew that Jonny's life would be different than that of a child who was not born with Down syndrome, and it's important for mothers of babies with Down syndrome to acknowledge that. But, there are lots of support groups everywhere—communities of people that help each other realize the joy associated with having a child with Down syndrome. My children are my teachers. I love them all, but my children with Down syndrome are truly lessons in love."

What If I Get Sick or Die?

I was so positive that I was finally pregnant that I took the pregnancy test the day before I was due to start my period! I had been trying to get pregnant for well over two years, and when it finally became a reality my mind-set immediately changed. Until that time I was consumed with getting pregnant, taking my temperature and having sex at the proper time. But when I finally did become pregnant, I immediately began to worry if I would be around as my daughter grew up.

As time went by the worries increased. I had my daughter when I was thirty-nine, and I felt fine. But then at forty-five began to have trouble with my back, started to see the first signs of menopause, and, in general, didn't feel like I did when I was younger. I woke up one day and realized my daughter was just six years old and I felt ninety. I attributed this to the fact that I never resumed my normal exercise program after my daughter was born. The truth is, that's when I began to write full time, and although I didn't blow up like a balloon, I did put on ten pounds and hardly ever exercised. Sitting in front of the computer for eight hours a day did not keep me in shape. My mind was exercising, but my body wasn't. I realized it was my responsibility to keep myself as healthy as I could, eat right and exercise, have a positive mental attitude, not only for myself, but so I could stay healthy for my child.

Many midlife mothers to whom I have spoken admit to feeling as if they have tempted fate by having a child later in life. My fear was most likely compounded by the fact that my own sister-in-law was diagnosed with cancer at age thirty-two, and for almost two years before I became pregnant with my youngest daughter, my family was faced with the possibility that she might die at a very young age. Her youngest son was only two at the time of her diagnosis, and I saw the pain and anguish her illness caused. But, it taught me that you can't predict the future, and being young when you have your children does not guarantee that you will be healthy as you raise them. I no longer feel that I have tempted fate by having a child at midlife. I have simply accepted that now is when I had her, and for us it was the best possible time.

Lack of Extended Family and Friends

Belinda Biori, a midlife mother at forty-seven years old, who lives in Los Angeles, California, confessed that, like me, she worried that she would not be around as her daughter grew up, but she was more worried that her child would have no extended family. Because of Belinda's advanced age when her daughter was born, the chances her child would have biological siblings was very small. Belinda's parents had already passed on. Her sister's kids, her daughter's cousins, were on their way to college. Belinda's daughter would not enjoy the extended family that Belinda loved as a child. "Some of my most fond memories are of my antics with my cousins around the holidays. I felt badly that my daughter wouldn't have that."

Belinda's solution was to get close friends involved. She looked to other families that live nearby who had also waited to have children and actually "chose" her extended family rather than depending on biology. "We have so much in common that we found ourselves going everywhere together. Both the adults and the children have grown very close, so we have vowed that we are now each other's extended family. The children call the adults 'auntie and uncle.' We spend the holidays together, and if there are ever disagreements we try to solve them quickly so we can maintain this close relationship."

Although traditional family values may be alive and well in our hearts, traditional families are quickly changing. The nuclear unit—the father, mother, and two-point-however-many children in which many of us grew up, has now given way to a variety of alternatives. (There are more kids in the U.S. living in stepfamilies than conventional two-parent homes.) Since we have made this choice to have children later in life, it's up to us to get a little creative and look past convention to find solutions. Belinda searched out good friends and created her own extended family. My friend Josie Bryant, who married a man twelve years younger and had her last child when she was well over the age of forty, had to give her own family a little pep talk.

"My husband's brothers and sisters have children the same age as the baby, and his parents are both under sixty years old, but everyone from my side of the family is much older. My sister's children have children the same age as my daughter, so the kids that my daughter will think of as her cousins are actually my grandnieces and nephews. But, family is family, and I wanted my daughter to be part of my family, old and new. At first my siblings didn't understand why this was such a big deal to me. I had to explain the importance of the extended family that we took for granted as kids, and then they became more supportive." Now Josie tells me that her family members also look for ways to help the younger ones be close to one another. "I don't think it really matters what order your relatives come in," Josie concluded. "Just that you have them and you are there for each other."

What Will the Neighbors Think?

Of course we all want support from friends and family for everything we do, and just because we're "big girls" and try to act like it doesn't make any difference if our loved ones don't support us in our decisions, of course it does. Not that the lack of support ever stopped me from going ahead and doing exactly what I pleased, but disapproval always registered.

I was surprised how strongly people felt about my decision to go forward with having a child at midlife. No one was on the fence. They were either right there with me, cheering me on, or they weren't.

"There are times when well-meaning friends are not kind," says Marissa Sorenson, a midlife mother who left a well-paying job to become a stay-at-home mom at the age of thirty-eight. "I had been married to my husband for two years. We were desperately trying to have a child. When I told my best friend, she asked, 'Are you stupid?' No support at all. She's no longer my best friend."

As I have already hinted, I had a very similar experience. One of my oldest friends made it painfully clear that she thought my decision to have a child "at my age" was ridiculous. Perhaps she was a little jealous of my lifestyle. She was bored in her marriage. She was bored with her life. Her children were in high school, her husband in and out of jobs. I had remarried a few years ago and had a lovely romantic relationship with my husband. Every other weekend our children from previous marriages went to their other parent's homes. We actually had two weekends a month we could be alone. My friend often asked, "Why would anyone want to ruin that with having more children?" I never saw it as ruining our marriage. I saw it as enhancing our marriage. Each month I cried when I didn't conceive and each month she told me how stupid I was for wanting a child. The experience didn't bring us closer.

In sharp contrast to today's midlife mothers, many of whom view having a child at midlife as a new beginning, midlife mothers of the past were often taken aback by the change in their life's plan and embarrassed by the notion of being pregnant when they were older. My good friend Florence La Bianco, a vibrant woman of seventy-four whose parents emigrated from Spain in the 1920s, had her only daughter at the young age of seventeen. She tells an interesting story about her own mother who had her last child at forty-five.

"My mother was forty-five when my youngest brother was born. I was fifteen, and the only girl. I had three older brothers when my younger brother was born. One day I heard a friend of my mother's whisper, 'Have you told the children yet?' 'Oh, no,' my mother shushed, and quickly waved her friend away. I had no idea what she was talking about until a few months later when my mother went to the hospital to have her baby. My poor mother, straight from Spain and very conservative, hid her pregnancy from her children. And my father supported her in her request. She was simply embarrassed. Can you imagine that? Not sharing a pregnancy with your daughter? In a household of men it could get rather lonely."

Are You the Grandma?

I will never forget the time my husband and I were invited to some new friends' house for dinner. Our daughter was about three months old. My husband walked in before me and began immediately chatting with his new friend. I was behind him carrying our baby. When the hostess, whom I had never met, saw me her hello comment was, "Oh, are you baby-sitting tonight? I didn't know you had grandchildren." My first reaction was to look over my shoulder. She couldn't be talking to me. In my mind I was a *brand-new* mother. Suddenly hundreds of questions filled my mind. Did I look like a grandmother? Was I old enough to be mistaken for a grandmother? Was I that much older than this woman? Was it time for that face-lift I had been talking about for the last few years? I didn't know how to respond so I just started laughing. "Uh, no," I replied. "This is *my* baby." I was thirty-nine.

"When my older son was about four years old and I was forty-five, I took him shopping to buy him character underwear and pajamas," said Jennifer Kendal, a stay-at-home mom who worked as a paralegal before her two children were born. "As I was paying for my merchandise, the salesgirl looked at me and said, 'Oh, is that your grandson? Are you watching him for the day?' 'No.' I said. 'This is my son.' And I shot her a look that could kill. I was so insulted, I could hardly think. Especially since I thought I looked young for my age. The salesgirl looked shocked and didn't know what to say, so it became a silent transaction."

The first time you are asked the "Grandma Question" it seems to hit you right square between the eyes. We're still in the new mommy mode, maybe even breast-feeding, a little sleep deprived, and someone throws a curve with this question. I would like to say it has happened only the one time, but I would be lying. As my daughter has gotten older, and therefore I have followed suit, it has happened now and again. But now I'm mentally prepared . . . and I think that's the key. I've learned that when someone throws a curve ball, you may have to change your stance in order to hit it. So, that's what I do. I stand up a little straighter, I smile a little brighter, and I have prepared some very poignant comebacks that require a snare drum for full impact.

Will My Child Think I Am Old?

Debbie DeDomenico is now well into her thirties and a bank manager. "When I was born, there were very few women as old as my mother still having babies," she explains. Her mother was forty-seven when Debbie was born. "I remember noticing that my parents were much older than my friends' parents, but I never got the sense that my parents were particularly *old*. I suppose my friends did. I remember when I was about ten being asked by a group of kids how old my father was. When I said fifty-eight, they were a little shocked. 'My grandfather is fifty-eight!' cried one little boy. I have to laugh because I remember thinking *he* was weird! My mother is still living. She's eighty years old. She is healthy and alert and now I am well into adulthood. I know my mom was always worried that she would pass on and leave me without a mother at an early age. I have friends younger than I who have lost their parents to illness or accident. I feel blessed I had the parents I had."

We are the ones who have the greatest impact on how our children perceive the concept of age. In Eastern cultures, parents and grandparents are respected for their wisdom and knowledge. It is believed that with age comes acute insight and increased intellect. It's only in the Western cultures that we chase down the Fountain of Youth, believing that we will gain some additional insight to life by staying young. The whole concept of age, for the young and old is stifling. We know that age is merely a chronological number rather than our true identity. "Old" is a state of mind. Rather than the word "old," why not bring up our children to see us as wise or experienced? What we project is what we will receive in return. If we don't think of ourselves as "old," then our children will not see us as "old" parents.

"I'm not sure little kids really understand the concept of age," suggests Reba Fisher, a forty-two-year-old stay-at-home-mom from McHenry, Illinois. "I remember a lady at our church asking her Sunday school class of preschoolers and kindergartners how old they thought she was on her last birthday. They said one hundred and six!"

Reba does have a point. I remember my own best friend's confusion when my father stopped going to work every morning. "Why is your dad staying home all the time?" she asked. "Is he sick?"

"No," I replied. "He's retired." I had no idea what retired meant. I was nine years old. That's just what my parents told me, so I just passed on the information. My friend then informed me that only *old* people retire and I began to panic. Was my father *old*? I was afraid to ask him.

A couple weeks later, my dad went back to work. He said he was bored and decided not to retire after all. I was relieved. "So you're not *old*?" I asked. He just laughed and scooped me onto his lap. I don't remember ever worrying about it again. I remember I was lucky enough to have a healthy father until he passed on at the age of seventy-eight. I was thirty-six years old.

While I was writing this book I often discussed the stories I was going to include with my younger sister, whom I am only admitting is younger for the sake of the following story. "Oh, I remember thinking Daddy was old," she explained. "He dropped off something when I was in third grade and one of my classmates asked if he was my grandpa. I was so embarrassed I just said yes. I didn't want to explain anything. To this day I feel badly that I said that."

I never thought of my midlife parents as old. *Old-fashioned*, maybe, but never old. However, I'm not sure if *every* child doesn't think of their parents as old-fashioned, children of midlife parents notwithstanding. The first time my oldest daughter, and I was twenty-nine when she was born, asked me how it was in the "olden days," it brought back memories of my asking my parents the same question. My husband, whose parents were a mere nineteen and twenty when he was born, has the same memory. It seems that being accused of being old-fashioned when you're a parent is sort of like having labor pain. Most of the time, it's inevitable. You may get through labor like life, with just a little discomfort, but that's usually only with the aid of medication, a great coach, or intense meditation . . .

Will I Pass on My Personal Demons?

When Diana Sloan was ten years old her mother was diagnosed with schizophrenia. Ten years ago her sister's oldest daughter began manifesting symptoms of the disease, and even though Diana was married, she made the decision then and there not to have biological children. Although Diana had no symptoms, she feared that she could pass on the disease that so plagued her mother and niece.

"I literally went into mourning for the children I would never have," Diana confided. "But, it was a decision I made for the love of them. You may think I overreacted to not want to have biological children, but I was there. I saw what this disease did to my mother—what it did to me as her child. I would rather die than to pass that on to my own children." Diana went on to explain that her fear of passing on mental illness stopped her from having biological children, but it did not squelch her desire to someday be a mother. After two years of red tape and attorney fees, she and her husband, Bill, adopted their son, Jack. "I wanted to raise children with Bill. I finally realized that I was afraid of my biology, but not of motherhood. It just took me some time to separate the two issues and figure it all out. Because of that, I'm an older mother, but I am confident I will be a better one now than I would have been when I was younger."

None of us enter this stage of our life without a past, and it takes work to embrace our mistakes and move through them to the next stage. After overcoming huge obstacles, Wendy, a midlife mom I met over the Internet who is pregnant for the first time at forty, talked to me about her fear of passing her alcoholism to her innocent baby. "As a recovering alcoholic I'm worried that my baby will inherit this disease. Plus, my husband is also recovering, and he has also been diagnosed with ADD. What kind of legacy are we passing on to this unsuspecting child?"

Wendy's concern is, of course, understandable. It is true that the ability to become an alcoholic is inherited, but the behavior associated with becoming an alcoholic is not. Wendy's children do not *have* to become alcoholics. Once she accepted that, she knew it was the right time to begin her family. She has told me that she will make it a point to teach her child right from the beginning that alcohol consumption in *their* family should be taken very seriously. "I watched my mother struggle with her own addiction and I see that as a warning of what not to do when I raise my own child," Wendy acknowledged. "I plan to make sure my child understands that he has a double-whammy, his dad and I are both recovering. We are living proof it's not something to play around with."

Am I Fit to Be a Mother?

Wendy went on to confess to an even greater fear that was also expressed by just about every midlife mom I spoke to. "This is my first. It's taken me a long time to get my life together. And, after all I have gone through to get here, what if I'm not a good mom?"

Concern about our ability to parent is normal and expected. Because we have waited so long for this blessed event, some fear that maybe they just won't make the grade. It goes without saying that jumping into motherhood without thinking it through is not a good idea, but for how long do you want to second-guess yourself and worry about your inabilities? Fear of the unknown will get you every time. The decision to have a child at any age breaks down to a mere leap of faith—faith in yourself, faith in your partner if you have one, and faith in knowing that humanity is actually capable of great things.

I found it interesting that Wendy chose the word "mom" instead of "mother" when admitting her concern about her future parenting skills. When a woman has a child, that woman is a mother. It's biology. A mother doesn't necessarily have to raise her own children. But, a mom is something different. Your mom is the person who rocks you when you are exhausted, celebrates your victories, cries at your losses. She doesn't have to be of the same blood, merely the same heart. It seems that Wendy inherently knew that being a mom is more than mere biology, and when I talked to her further it became quite obvious that her true fear was that she would not be close to this child for whom she waited so long.

"Alcohol played such a huge part in my upbringing," Wendy confided. "I always felt like an afterthought to my mother. First there was alcohol, and then there was Wendy. I don't ever want my child to feel like that."

No parent does everything right. Although we would like to believe we do, we are human, and with that humanness comes the capacity to make mistakes. If you are sincerely concerned about your ability to parent, that just means you will try even harder to do what's right. If you had a troubled upbringing, your parents made bad choices, then it's up to you to make different choices when you have children. You are not doomed to re-create their mistakes. Go to counseling, read books that teach positive methods to deal with stress and decision making, make sure you attend your AA meetings, talk to friends, your minister, or rabbi. Interact with your children's teachers. Use every avenue open to you to help guide you through the process. And, if you have done the best you can, then you can let go of your fear of being a bad parent. We are all a work in progress.

Silly Fears

Expectant mothers have forty weeks to wait for a child. It's not uncommon for adoptive mothers to wait even longer. In that time, our minds can run wild worrying about silly things that have no effect on the health or quality of life of our children. "I worried about the same thing when pregnant with all my children," said Robin, a midlife mom from rural Pennsylvania who tells me the town she lives in is so small it only has one stoplight. "This may sound stupid, but I have a huge fear that my kids will be ugly. Isn't that awful? It's sort of a joke in the family now, especially between my oldest daughter and me. Every day she sees my son she says, Oh look at him! He's getting cuter!"

I had my own silly fear. I had a secret wish that my daughter wouldn't inherit my mother's legs as I did. One day I was joking about that with my mom. She didn't take offense, but she did put me in my place. "I think I would concentrate on hoping she is born with my beautiful eyes and superior intellect, and not worry about my legs."

As it was, my daughter was born with her beautiful eyes, her superior intellect, and her ankles. She was spared the legs.

Calming Serious Fears

The consensus of opinion from most of the midlife mothers that I interviewed is this: Put everything in place—set up a college fund, or draw up a will, make an agreement where your child will live should something happen to you, and then relax and enjoy it. Agonizing about your age or your life situation will rob you of the pleasure of raising your child. Days will slip by without grace. And the one thing on which all midlife mothers agree is that time passes without our consent. I can't count how many midlife moms have told me, "I woke up, and I was forty."

Many of us have learned to accept and appreciate our gift rather than worry about what is unforeseen. "I guess I have all the same, typical worries as everyone else," explains Sue, who at forty-one just found out she was having twins. "I became pregnant, not trying, and so it's been tough. I'm forty-one and my husband is fifty-three. He has less a problem with age then me."

"Of course, I was worried, but my last ultrasound showed all good things. We opted to not have an amnio. It's late in my pregnancy, anyway. I'm twenty-three weeks. I guess I'm just turning it over to a Higher Power, and I know that things will be okay. My mom was thirty-five when she had me. She is the greatest. She's supportive, loving, caring, and there whenever I need her. She cries, laughs, and jokes with me about everything. I feel very blessed to have her."

Sue has no apprehension about having a child at midlife because she is the child of a midlife mother and knows it to be a positive experience. Her mom laid the groundwork, and she will most likely be an inspirational grandmother to Sue's child, just as she is a "living inspiration" to Sue. What better inheritance can we offer our children than to be an inspirational role model? To pass on qualities such as strength of character, dignity, and courage is truly our greatest legacy. Perhaps it is human nature to worry about the unknown, but it is also human nature to explore new territories, and forge new trails, "to go where no other person has gone before," all qualities of today's midlife mother. It's no accident that Sue became a mother at midlife, and her children are sure to reap the benefits.

Perhaps calming our worries is best put into perspective by Katherine Weiss, who at age forty-five became a single mom for the first time. "To me, my son is a marvel," says Katherine. "I look at him when he sleeps, so peaceful, so lovable, and I wonder why I waited for so long to have him. I have never felt unconditional love, nor been able to give it, but when my son was born I finally understood what my place was. Granted, I was forty-five years old, but my direction was clear and I am at peace."

THREE

The Challenges of Waiting—Our Race Against Time

"My friend called to share her good news the other day. This is the same friend that started out going through infertility with me fifteen years ago. She's expecting her fourth child. I am so happy for her. Honestly."

—PAULA GIMELLI, STILL TRYING TO CONCEIVE

Women who delay childbearing know they may have to pay the consequences. They may have to take pills to increase ovulation, or have operations to clear scar tissue, fertilize eggs outside their bodies, and even ask others to carry their children for them. Because of the advances in medical science, cures to problems that were evasive even twenty years ago are now easily detected, and couples who could only dream of becoming biological parents can now experience the miracle of conception, pregnancy, and childbirth. Nevertheless, the road to having a child at midlife is sometimes a bumpy one. There are those of us that get pregnant without help from technology, but statistics tell us that after the age of thirty-five one in five women will have trouble conceiving. More and more, we have to admit the grim reality—infertility, to some degree, is simply a byproduct of midlife parenthood. It's a race against time.

As I spoke to midlife mothers about their struggles to have children, I found there were two things felt by most at some point in their quest to evade infertility. First, bewilderment. Why did this happen to me? Why can't *I* have children? And, second, guilt. Whether the mother was punishing herself for waiting "too long" or feeling guilty about a past too frivolous for condoms, guilt was somewhere in the equation, and dealing with that guilt became just as much of an issue as the infertility itself.

The stories volunteered on the following pages are from women who have fought the midlife infertility battle. Many of them have gone on to have biological children, both with and without medical intervention. Others have chosen to adopt. These are *our* midlife warriors, and their stories are as uplifting as the women who tell them.

Mary Larsen is a petite woman with dark hair that curls all around her face. She's a touch overweight, but on her it looks good. We agreed to meet at the park near her home, and she told me the story of how she finally got pregnant while her two-year-old son pushed toy trucks through the sand near her feet. As soon as we began talking she exhibited a touch of her dry sense of humor—the kind that belongs on *Saturday Night Live*. I simply asked her how long she had been married.

"I used to hate that question." She laughed. "When someone asked how many years my husband and I have been married, I would answer, 'Seven years' . . . and they would say, 'Seven years? And, no kids?' And, then I would want to reach over the table, grab their little neck, and strangle them." She mimicked putting her hands around someone's neck and shaking it back and forth. She stopped the antics, remembering her son at her feet, and patted him on the head to reassure him everything was fine. "I was *trying*, damn it."

She continued, still with the same tone to her voice. "I didn't want kids. I was a working woman! I loved my job, but like so many other women of my generation, I hit forty and the alarm went off. And then I couldn't get pregnant if I wanted to. My husband almost left—he couldn't stand me anymore. I had about a week each month when I was civil, then I would anticipate ovulation, get anxious, start having anxiety attacks, I was about ready for the loony bin. I decided enough was enough. I made an appointment with a therapist and with his guidance I was introduced to the fertility clinic that helped us conceive our child. But the stress was too much. I could not do it again."

Mary Larsen's problem was easily diagnosed. At forty-two she was beginning to experience the first signs of menopause. Her hormones were running rampant—the reason for the mood swings, but her specialist worked with her, prescribed the proper medication, and that's when Mary conceived her now two-year-old son Sam.

"I'm right in the throes of menopause now. No way I could ever have another child. Thank God it wasn't too late for us."

I'm Infertile? Me?

When I met Lisa McCall, I swear I thought she was thirty and I almost told her she was too young to be included in this book. Lisa is forty-two years old and lives in San Jose, California, the heart of Silicon Valley, with her husband, Roy. She goes to the gym every day and runs four miles three times a week. You may wonder why couldn't someone so healthy get pregnant?

"I tried to get pregnant for over a year," Lisa told me. "When nothing happened I decided to stop my regular exercise routine. I thought, maybe it was all the exercise."

A regular exercise program is not the reason an average woman cannot conceive. You have to train for hours a day, and have extremely low body fat; menstruation may even stop before exercise is the culprit. Very few women actually have the time to exercise enough to where their fertility comes into question. Lisa was looking for any excuse other than her body could not conceive. We all do that. Maybe it's the water I drink, maybe it's stress, maybe I'm not a nice enough person. Many women are convinced that if the outside hasn't aged, the inside hasn't either. That's not the way it works.

In Lisa's case, because she was older, her hormone levels were declining and she needed a little help in order to ovulate on a regular basis.

"I never gave any thought to ovulation." Lisa shrugged. "To me it was all just part of the process each month. Not until I was desperate to get pregnant did I start taking my temperature and charting my ovulation. I found I never ovulated at the same time each month. *I* ovulated irregularly? Me?"

For some there are warning signs of impending infertility—painful intercourse, extremely heavy or light periods, pain for no apparent reason, irregular periods. For others, the discovery that they are infertile comes as a complete surprise. The truth is between 20 and 30 percent of all female infertility patients, not just women at midlife trying to conceive, experience problems with ovulation or other hormonal imbalances. In order to find the reason behind the infertility a complete infertility work up should be performed. It's long and tedious testing. In Lisa's case, the drug Clomid was prescribed. She would then not only ovulate on time, but also have the increased chance of conceiving twins. "That wouldn't be so bad." Lisa laughed. "We could take it."

My Story

Like so many couples at midlife, my husband and I had both been previously married and had children. After my husband's second child was born, he had a vasectomy. For us to have children, he would have to have his vasectomy surgically reversed.

Although a vasectomy reversal is microscopic surgery, when his urologist explained the procedure it seemed simple enough, and I was very excited about having a baby. When I didn't get pregnant immediately after the procedure was done, I just knew it was because the reversal had failed, and I resented my husband beyond belief. I hated everybody. A sperm count revealed my husband had a healthy sperm count even for a man who had never had a vasectomy. The fault was mine! I was humbled, to say the least.

The shock of my life was finding out I could no longer have children. I already had one. She was a healthy nine-year-old. My previous pregnancy was trouble free. I did have a cesarean, but that was because my daughter was footling breech and my ob/gyn decided it was too risky to try a vaginal birth. It never dawned on me that something could have happened over the years that would prevent me from having another child. Those things happen to someone else. It's the kind of story your girlfriend whispers over coffee about another girlfriend. You both feel terrible, but you know it will never happen to you. So after a year and a half of taking my temperature and crying each time I started my period, plus proof positive that my husband's vasectomy reversal was successful, my doctor suggested a diagnostic laparoscopy. I was already taking fertility drugs to guarantee ovulation. "If you were younger I would prescribe stronger fertility drugs and see what happens," he said. "But I don't want to waste any time."

When I told this story to Elena, a woman well into her forties who also fought midlife infertility, she smiled. "Same thing happened to me. I guess we could have messed around with a lot of drugs before they checked surgically, but since I was forty-two, they went in to see what was wrong."

"And what was wrong?" I asked.

"Nothing. At least that's what they said. They couldn't find a thing wrong. They suggested we keep trying. And we did. It took us four years to conceive. After the laparoscopy, we did start drug therapy." She was holding her one-year-old son on her lap as we spoke. "But the hormones made me feel very emotional. At least I blamed it on the hormones. I'm glad it's over."

> **Midlife Mom Memo:**
> What is a diagnostic laparoscopy? A laparoscope, which resembles a pencil-thin telescope with a light at the end, is inserted through a tiny incision near the belly button. A physician can then see inside the abdomen and hopefully discover the reason behind the infertility.

In my case, when the diagnostic laparoscopy was performed, it was found that I had developed endometriosis, a condition that over time causes scar tissue to form around the Fallopian tubes, ovaries, and uterus. In rare cases the uterine wall and even the bowel is affected. Because of the scarring, it is very difficult to become pregnant.

Research tells us that endometriosis is more common in women entering midlife who have never had children, but science has yet to pinpoint the exact reason this is true. For me, the diagnostic laparoscopy did the trick. My doctor pinpointed the endometriosis, used a laser to remove it, and I became pregnant the next month. Although we have never used birth control since the birth of our daughter, I never got pregnant again.

Miscarriage: Coping with Loss

Having a miscarriage is difficult to accept in itself, but if you are battling midlife infertility, a miscarriage is particularly devastating. And, since fathers often relate to miscarriage quite differently than mothers, a woman can feel understandably alone in her grief.

Let me explain further. To the father, early pregnancy is sort of surreal. Unlike the mother, he is not feeling hormonal changes or morning sickness. He knows the mother is pregnant because he has been told, but until the mother starts looking pregnant, the baby is just a dream. Because he may not have fully identified with the pregnancy, when the mother has an early miscarriage, he may appear insensitive about the loss.

It's not uncommon, however, for the mother to think of that early pregnancy as a baby. We all know that a baby starts from an egg and a sperm and does not become recognizable for weeks after conception, but when you imagine your child, no matter how far along you are, you imagine a fully formed little person, not a blob of cells. Some women immediately personalize the pregnancy, and that's why it may be more difficult for a woman than a man to deal with loss through early miscarriage.

"I just wanted him to be a little upset that we lost the baby, but he seemed more bewildered than anything else," said Lori, who at thirty-nine has been battling infertility for three years. She was talking about her husband, Jeff. "His attitude was, We'll keep trying. He even said, It wasn't like it was a real baby. But it was to me, so I'm having a tough time with it. I'm on a runaway emotion roller coaster and I'm not sure how to stop it."

"Well, maybe it was meant to be," or "That's nature's way," or "There could have been something wrong with the baby," and "it's probably for the best," are common comments after miscarriage.

Although well-intentioned, these comments rarely help the grieving mother. The problem is, people who care about you don't know what to say to make you feel better, and so in their quest for the right words, they say what they think is appropriate. Lori's own husband didn't know what to say. Perhaps the best course of action is to have a frank discussion with friends and relatives about how you are feeling after a miscarriage. Explain that it is a difficult time for you, and then go about the business of mourning your loss. Remember, mourning and grief are necessary steps to dealing with miscarriage, and, thankfully, after a period of adjustment, it is basic to human nature to want to look ahead.

A Woman's Guilt and Infertility

Midlife Mom Memo:

Salpingitis, the technical term for the scarring of the Fallopian tubes, accounts for more than 30 percent of all female infertility problems.

Scarred Fallopian tubes and pelvic inflammatory disease (PID) are common causes of infertility in woman at mid-life, and there is good reason. As you approach forty, most women have had more than one or two sexual partners. If you have not practiced safe sex in the past, this puts you at risk for an undetected sexually transmitted disease. Some STDs (sexually transmitted diseases) have no warning signs. You could have the infection such as chlamydia, a cross between a bacterial and viral disease, which has few or no symptoms, and not even know it. Then, say ten years later, you decide to have a baby and you can't get pregnant because your Fallopian tubes have been scarred. The blockages will not permit conception and you are diagnosed with pelvic inflammatory disease. The guilt that some women feel from the knowledge that their past behavior may have contributed to their infertility can be just as overwhelming as the infertility diagnosis.

Astrid was fourteen the first time she went to a music concert. "To this day my parents have no idea I went. I look back on those days and think if my daughter ever did half of the things I did, oh my. We were so open, so free. The thought that someone might hurt me never crossed my mind." Astrid shook her head. "I can't believe we were all that stupid, but it's what I did. And, about two weeks after the concert I ended up with a terrible case of gonorrhea. I have no excuse but immaturity and ignorance. I had no idea what I was doing, and that one day played havoc with the rest of my life."

As you can well imagine, Astrid did not know that she had gonorrhea and she was afraid to tell her mother that something was wrong. "I can't remember how long I had it, but not long after the concert, a friend with a car said she was going to Planned Parenthood. I asked her what Planned Parenthood was and she explained that they would talk to us about birth control and not tell our parents. I went with her, and as part of the procedure, a doctor examined me. I think about this now and I can't believe it was me. Of course, the proper medicines were prescribed, but I believe that is what started my infertility problem. Perhaps I'm wrong, but I don't think so."

"I never even knew I had an infection," says Trisha Madden, a forty-year-old flight attendant who has been married to the same man for over a decade. "I certainly have never had one in the last twelve years, so it must have been before I met and married my husband. I did use an IUD (intrauterine device) for birth control, but that was so long ago. You mean I did something that many years ago that could possibly jeopardize my now having children?"

Midlife Mom Memo:

The IUD is the most inexpensive long-term reversible method of contraception available in the world. Unfortunately, years of negative publicity and speculation following lawsuits brought on by the sale and use of a faulty IUD—the Dalkon Shield—raised many questions about the safety of all IUDs. IUDs were blamed for the rise of PID in the U.S. Some manufacturers even withdrew safe IUDs from the American market. The IUD is still recognized by the World Health Organization, the American Medical Association, and the American College of Obstetricians and Gynecologists as one of the safest and most effective reversible methods of birth control for women. This, however, is after years of trial and research.

Finding a Cure

Infertility is best treated with a dual approach, both medically *and* psychologically—first, deciding the proper medical treatment and then searching out a therapist who is familiar with treating women coping with infertility. From a psychological point of view, infertility can be particularly difficult to treat. Just when the patient begins to make progress, they are reminded by the onset of their period that they again have not succeeded in achieving their final goal. The stress this creates truly complicates the condition.

Trisha Madden agrees. "Every month at the first sign of menstruation I would feel like such a failure, so guilty that this was my fault. I would secretly lock myself in the bathroom so no one would know how depressed I was and I would cry until I couldn't breathe. I have never told my husband what caused the blockage in my Fallopian tubes. I was too embarrassed to discuss the possibilities. I can't go there."

After four years of trying to conceive and two diagnostic laparoscopies, Trisha became pregnant at age forty-four. Daniel Wayne Madden was born twenty-one days premature, weighing five pounds one ounce. As of this writing, Astrid Jones has been unable to conceive and is looking into adopting a child.

Finding a Specialist

If you are ready to confront infertility, your first step is to find an infertility specialist with whom you feel comfortable.

* **START BY ASKING YOUR GYNECOLOGIST.** Although she can perform many of the tests necessary to locate the reason behind your infertility, a specialist has had additional training in the field and devotes most of her time to solving specific infertility problems. Your gynecologist may work closely with a particular group of specialists and can easily suggest someone in whom she has confidence.

* **YOUR FRIENDS AND FAMILY ARE AN EXCELLENT RESOURCE.** If your problem is inherited, it is likely someone in your family has already addressed the same problem and can offer the name of a specialist.

* **LOCAL HOSPITALS AND COMMUNITY MEDICAL CLINICS** often have infertility referral services, and try the yellow pages for specialists right in your neighborhood.

* **DON'T FORGET THE INTERNET.** If your goal is to find out everything about your condition, use the key word "infertility" and you will find volumes of information, support groups, even chat rooms on the subject.

* **DON'T TRUST THE NATIONAL AVERAGE QUOTED FOR SUCCESS RATES.** Once you find a specialist you like, ask her in person what her success rate is for the particular procedure you require. That will give you an accurate assessment of her expertise and personal success rate. You may also want to discuss how your health care professional screens her patients. If the clinic only takes low-risk patients, for example, success rates may be inflated.

* **THE CENTERS FOR DISEASE CONTROL AND PREVENTION (CDC)** offers a yearly study about the success rates of assisted reproductive technology (ART). This study is available on the Internet and offers reliable statistics from all ART procedures reported. For contact information for the CDC, please refer to the resource guide at the back of this book.

QUESTIONS TO ASK IN PICKING A SPECIALIST

1. What is your success rate for this procedure? Out of 100, how many are *not* successful? This number will allow you to quickly calculate his rate of success.

2. How many times have you performed this operation?

3. How long will the procedure take?

4. Will you use a general or local anesthesia?

5. Will this procedure be covered by insurance?

If you would like to speak directly with agencies dedicated to combating infertility, please check at the resource guide at the back of this book.

Adoption as an Answer

Adoption is not the answer for everyone, but it was for Melinda and Wayne Willis. One autumn afternoon at the age of thirty-five, Melinda became a mom, diaper bag and all. However, her journey to motherhood began many years before.

Married to her husband Wayne at twenty, and both on the verge of graduation from college, they had lots of dreams for the future—jobs, children, and travel adventures. When their friends began to have children, they courageously responded that they were waiting. They had plenty of time for that later. Right now they were more interested in job security and establishing themselves as "real" grown-ups. Plenty of time.

Shortly after Wayne got his first job teaching at a college, Melinda began in earnest to consider having a child. They had no idea that either of them had any physical problems that might affect their pursuit. Soon that would all change. Over the course of the next three years, both underwent surgery, tried various medications and methods to attempt to become pregnant, changed doctors, but with no success. Finally in the spring of 1987, they made the final visit to a fertility specialist at Duke University to be told that they would probably never be able to conceive a child together.

"I still remember that day," says Melinda. "What I was wearing, the look on Wayne's face, the numbness of walking back to the car, the feeling of powerlessness to change anything, the long, silent drive back home. It seemed like our parenting dream had come to an end."

For the next three years, they sort of danced around the issue, which became a huge problem that almost drove them apart. Melinda found it impossible to escape what she felt was an innate need to be a mother, and Wayne's need for privacy would not allow sharing their situation with even their closest friends. "I spent a lot of time wondering to myself how to go about reconciling these maternal urges with the reality of infertility. This struggle was very difficult and one that I had to face alone."

Counseling helped them to come to grips with ways to be appreciative of each other's needs. They became more at ease with their infertility issues, and slowly shared their plight with their trusted friends, whom they found to be sympathetic and sensitive. With this additional support they were able to weigh their options regarding parenthood "out loud" and benefited from their friends' suggestions and connections.

The truth was they *did* have choices they could make. One was artificial insemination with another man's sperm, an option that neither Wayne nor Melinda felt comfortable considering. Ironically, like so many infertile couples weighing the possibilities, Wayne and Melinda felt more comfortable with the option of raising a child who was in no way biologically related than a child that was biologically related to only one of them. Adoption was their final decision.

Finally, after years from start to finish, they adopted a little girl. "The arrival of this child into my world was more than I had expected," says Melinda. "I had never known such joy or experienced such wonder at this tiny life I'd been given to care for and love. After all that we'd been through, getting up at 2 A.M. was a delight, a chance to hold our daughter and each other and marvel at the miracle of the moment. Wayne would dance with her in the kitchen while I prepared her late-night snack. I just didn't worry a lot about what kind of diapers to buy, being on a strict schedule, the shape of the bottle's nipple, and the "right" stroller with all the latest options. I found myself taking the time to point out the wild violets along the road as we walked/strolled. We watched cooking shows on television and then went to the kitchen to prepare dinner—she was in her baby carrier, kicking away; I was telling her about the differences between stirring and folding. As a result of my educational background in child development, I was amazed at her early language development, her attempts at making humor, her curiosity about the world around her. I refused to have a playpen in the house, believing that she needed a chance to explore and move about at will. She was 'late' learning to go to sleep on her own because we loved rocking her to sleep so much."

Yet, even as they were aware of the fulfillment of their dreams and celebrated each landmark event in their daughter's young life, the realities of sleep deprivation and limited financial resources began to wear them down. "I had never known such weariness or experienced such frustration at the lack of closure involved in parenting," Melinda confided.

Perhaps the most dramatic realization for Melinda was related to the notion that as an adoptive parent she should somehow be more patient, more loving, and more grateful for this child than other parents who had come by their children the "regular" way. "I was constantly beating myself up emotionally because I thought I had been given a more precious gift than other mothers. One of my wise friends who had her kids the 'regular' way said to me, 'Melinda, once you brought that baby into your home, you are just a regular mom like the rest of us. She is your daughter, just like Lindsey is my daughter. Neither you nor she is any more special than any other family. Just relax and be normal like the rest of us—delight in the new things she does, brag a little, get frustrated, and be tired. You are a mom.'

"And a mom I am and I am becoming. As an adoptive parent I understand that the environment I provide for my daughter to grow and become in is only part of who she is. Many ways of hers are hereditary and mostly outside of my control. Other 'regular' parents are also in the same situation, but I'm not sure that they are as keenly aware of these kinds of subtleties. I also live with the knowledge that someday she will probably want to locate her birth parents. Presently,

I'm perfectly okay with that possibility. Like her, I too am curious and want to know about the whole picture, the details."

The love for his daughter lead Dr. Wayne Willis, Melinda's husband, to write a wonderful book for children about their adoption called *This Is How We Became a Family*. It is the story of a couple who long for a child, a pregnant young woman who is not ready to raise her baby, and the events that bring them together for a happy ending. The dedication reads, "To Susannah . . . and every other child who was ever the answer to someone's hopes, dreams, or prayers."

Overcoming Infertility: Triumph!

I couldn't write a book about becoming a mother at midlife without including Annette's story. Annette has been one of my best friends since junior high school. She was a partner in crime, the kind of friend that even if we don't talk for years we pick right up where we left off.

Our lives travel in a curious parallel, and when my own infertility fight was at its peak, her son wasn't quite two years old. I called her to cry on her shoulder. I couldn't get pregnant and I was devastated. Little did I know that in order to have her handsome Dylan, Annette had waged her own battle with infertility. She endured eight miscarriages and finally after finding a doctor she believes is a miracle worker, carried her son to term. But, by that time, my dear friend Annette was thirty-seven years old.

"Sometimes I look at him," Annette told me, "and, I still don't believe I have a son. It's simply so amazing, miscarriage after miscarriage, I didn't think it was possible."

This woman will turn anything into a joke—the more irreverent, the better. Right now, she was laughing at herself. "I started to think I was doomed, you know. Not just bad things were happening to me.

Full-fledged doomed. Like the grim reaper was standing at my door saying, 'Annette, I'm sorry, but we're not going to let you have children this time around. Maybe next life. This one, you're screwed.' "

She was laughing again, this time in disbelief. "Everyone was pregnant, you know? It didn't matter where I turned. The woman next door, grocery checkers, both of my sisters were pregnant . . . at the same time! I couldn't handle it."

Her expression changed. She talks with her hands and she folded them in front of her, holding her elbows and leaning toward me as she spoke. "I remember being on a family picnic and completely miserable around my two pregnant sisters. I'm the middle sister. There's a whole psychological thing associated with my older sister *and* my younger sister both being pregnant. That's another therapy session." Annette often makes "time-to-go-to-therapy" jokes about herself, but now she was serious, passing on an unpleasant memory. "The whole thing was just so typical of the way my life has gone. Nothing has ever been easy. Anyway, we're at this picnic and my youngest sister said, 'If you want a kid so bad, you can just have one of mine.' Like she had extras and she would just give me one of hers. I know it was just a flip comment, but it was the wrong flip comment. My dad saw the look on my face and snapped, 'Leave her alone! Annette will have her own children!' My dad very rarely says things like that and I realized I was upsetting my whole family. It was time to get some therapy. And, therapy did help for a while."

Annette took a deep breath. "But, I swear to God if my therapist didn't turn up pregnant, too! Here I am spilling my guts, telling her week after week how badly I felt after each miscarriage, that everyone around me is pregnant, and you know how a therapist will greet you at the door, then guide you to your chair? Well, this time she was walking sort of funny. I think she was trying to hide her belly! We started the session, but I couldn't stand it. 'Are you pregnant?' I asked her. All she could say was, 'Yes.'

"Well you could have hit me over the head with a brick! My God, how long had she known? Week after week, I talked to her and she never said a thing. She did suggest I go see a doctor at Stanford. Later I figured out she must have been seeing him, too. That was another wasted year and a half."

"You must have felt terrible!" I said. I could only imagine.

"I felt completely betrayed. My own therapist, pregnant. I was done!"

That's when Annette came across Dr. Alan Beer. "Hope was gone," Annette told me, her voice uncharacteristically calm. "But somehow Dr. Beer figured it out."

Dr. Alan Beer, an innovator in the field of reproductive immunology, has helped thousands of couples deliver healthy babies since 1970. His treatment is still controversial, but it's based on the idea that miscarriages are often caused by a problem with the immune system. Through his Reproductive Medicine Program, with offices in northern California and Chicago, Dr. Beer is committed to helping couples that have experienced recurrent miscarriages, multiple pregnancy losses, or repeated in vitro fertilization failures achieve a successful pregnancy. That was Annette. She fit the profile perfectly. And, when she heard that Dr. Beer testified to achieving successful pregnancies in approximately 85 percent of the couples he has treated, she wasted no time in contacting him.

"I really don't care what his critics say. I had miscarriage after miscarriage. I doubted myself. I doubted my marriage. I harbored an incredible amount of guilt because I knew the infertility was my fault. It was the only way that I could have had a son."

She handed me her son's latest picture, beaming from ear to ear. He's eleven years old, and he looks exactly like her.

"Thank God, for Dr. Beer."

Midlife Mom Memo:

In vitro fertilization (IVF) uses fertility drugs to stimulate the ovaries into producing several eggs per cycle. The eggs are retrieved through surgery, fertilized by sperm in a dish, and then the embryos are transferred into the mother's uterus. When women are approaching forty and older, doctors are more aggressive with the fertility drugs to increase the number of eggs, therefore offering a greater number of viable eggs to be fertilized. There is a better success rate for woman under forty—28.7 births per 100 as opposed to 8.7 births per 100 for women over forty. IVF can be very expensive and since the rate of success is so much less for women at midlife, some IVF clinics actually limit the number of women they accept as potential candidates.

I remember when the first baby was born by in vitro fertilization in 1978. My mom and I were driving in the car listening to talk radio. There was a break for news, the announcement was made, and my mother's face went pale. "What's happening to our world?" she asked. Even though I was in my early twenties, I wasn't sure exactly what they were talking about, but when my mom explained it to me—an egg fertilized by a sperm in a petri dish, then transferred into the mother's womb. The mental image I created was not at all like what we think of in vitro fertilization today. The news flash prompted a conversation about *Brave New World*, a book my mother had not read, and she was sure it was completely inappropriate that I had read it. I explained to her that it was required reading in the eighth grade. She shook her head in disbelief. "Well, I didn't know you were reading that stuff."

Thinking back and picturing myself in the car with my mother, it doesn't seem that long ago. When I did the math, I realized that in less than twenty-five years, rather than shake our heads in disapproval, it is taken for granted that in vitro fertilization is a possible choice for couples who cannot conceive by conventional methods.

Janet Nunan and her husband, Patrick, are one of those couples. They had been trying to conceive for seven years. Janet had suffered through ten tries using in vitro fertilization, each time was a grim reminder that she could not carry a baby to term. Susie Kevorkian is Janet's best friend. Susie and Janet met in their late twenties while both were serving on a charity fund-raising committee. As I sat in Susie's living room eating homemade soup and juggling Janet's fifteen-week-old twins, Libby and Max, I had no idea the effect this story would have on me.

"Well," Susie began. "I guess it started with dinner. Janet and I were working together for a charity and I invited her and her husband, Patrick, for dinner. Patrick almost said no. He didn't want to deal with any more Junior League stuff and he was tired.

"They did come over that night, and our friendship was born. My husband, Kevin, and Patrick got along great. Janet and Patrick became the friends with whom we did everything. Then it got to the time in our marriages when we both wanted to have children. I couldn't imagine having children without Janet as part of their lives. Well, I got pregnant with my first child, and Janet and Patrick were trying. I got pregnant with my second child and Janet and Patrick were still trying. By the third, it was heartbreaking. I'd be talking to Janet on the phone and she would be crying. When you are friends with someone and your friend is suffering, you want to be able to take their pain away. We all felt helpless. Eventually, they found there was something wrong with the lining of her uterus. She did get pregnant, but she couldn't carry the babies. She finally tried in vitro fertilization. Eleven times! And, every time she cried, my heart broke with her."

Now it was Janet's turn. "We decided to go on a vacation together. Susie was pregnant with her third child, Annie, and Patrick and I had begun to seriously consider adoption. We had already started doing research on adoption agencies when Susie and Kevin sat down with us and offered to carry our child. Susie said, 'Kevin and I want to do this for you.'"

My first impression was that Janet must have been elated, but that wasn't her reaction at all. "No, I wasn't," Janet admitted. "My first reaction was, 'Absolutely not!' I love Susie and it was just too big of a responsibility. If it didn't work, *both* Susie and I would be devastated. I couldn't ask her to set herself up for such disappointment. I couldn't be responsible for her disappointment, too."

"I had to convince her." Susie laughed. "I was on the phone every day telling her that after Annie was born, I was ready."

"It just wasn't that easy," Janet explained. She and Patrick had spent well over two hundred thousand dollars trying to conceive over the last seven years. The amount it would cost to do the transfer was exactly the amount it would cost to adopt. And, adopting was a sure thing.

"It finally got to the point where I gave her a due date," said Susie. "I said I'm offering you this until January, but then I have to get on with my life. If I'm going to be pregnant again, I don't want to try to diet and lose weight. I want to eat well and be as healthy as I can for the transfer. I reminded her that she was never going to get an offer like this again. Plus, she already had frozen embryos waiting."

"But there were other considerations," Janet added. "Susie gets a condition at the end of each pregnancy. It's a problem with her liver, almost as if she gets chicken pox on the inside. She knew she would get the condition again, and it makes it very difficult for her to get around. She had just been pregnant and went through eight weeks of liver problems. I knew if she did this, she would get sick. And, being pregnant again so soon could wreak havoc with her marriage. I was concerned on so many different levels."

Susie agreed. She didn't know all the emotional implications of being a surrogate, nor did she understand the legal implications. Her husband, Kevin, is a lawyer, so that made that part much easier, but they soon learned that in order for the transfer of babies to be legal, Janet and Patrick would have to sue for custody of their own biological babies. That was amazing to me. Not knowing that much about the legality of surrogacy, I assumed she was telling me that legal custody of a baby lies with the birth mother . . . but in this case, the birth mother may not be the one who gives birth. I had never thought about the possibility of law being impacted by advancements in medical science. It certainly was a good thing Susie's husband was a lawyer.

"I'm a stay-at-home mom," continued Susie. "I knew that if I was going to take this on I was going to need help. In my mind, I had devised a plan of how it would work, but it was a big step for Janet. She would have to quit her job and in essence become a surrogate mother to my children. While I carried the baby, she would have to help me take care of my kids."

Janet mimicked a look of bewilderment. "Susie was so convinced. She had it all figured out. I was trying to digest it all."

"So," Susie continued. "That's exactly what she did. She was here every day after school. She drove the car pools. She cooked the dinners. The kids got so they depended on her and couldn't wait to see her."

Janet was nodding in agreement. It was obvious that she, too, had built a strong bond with Susie and Kevin's children. "I love them."

So, six weeks after Susie's daughter Annie was born, Susie and Janet's specialist attempted an IVF transfer. Exactly what Janet feared would happen, did. The transfer was not successful. Janet was devastated. "Now, I was really finished."

"But, I was fine with it," said Susie. "I hadn't gone through all the disappointment Janet had, and I was raring to go again." Susie laughed. "What's one try? Let's do it again! I convinced her, but this time we used a live transfer rather than frozen embryos."

"And, you're holding Max." Susie smiled.

"The babies are wonderful," Janet said softly. "But we received far more than the babies. To grow as close to another family as we have become, to cry with each other, to care for each other's children. Having these babies was a wonderful favor that Susie and Kevin gave us, but to do it with such grace and kindness. The journey was really the wonderful part. The path we walked to get to the babies was the real blessing."

DONOR EGGS

Thanks to medical assistance more and more women are able to have children as they approach midlife. While some conceive using their own eggs, others choose to use eggs donated by someone else. This causes a whole new set of problems for the new mother.

"I don't know if you are interested in my particular story. I wound up having to use donor eggs. If you are going to bash me for my choice, please don't even write back."

That was my first communication with Maria, a midlife mother I met through an Internet e-group I joined when doing research for this book. "Hmmm," I thought. "Do people actually give her a hard time for using donor eggs?" At this point I had talked to so many women fighting the infertility battle at midlife, I thought using donor eggs was a great idea if it would actually allow you to carry a child to term. Maria and I continued to E-mail back and forth for over three months. She is an amazingly loving and gentle soul. Here is her story. Maria was thirty-nine when she sent this to me. Her precious son, Juan, was two years old.

"To be honest, I had never encountered prejudice and judgment before in my life. It came as a shock. After the journey I had traveled, to receive that kind of response was very difficult for me. I needed support and validation. I think it stems from ignorance. If you have not experienced infertility firsthand, you cannot possibly understand the emotion or the choices. Some women are very conservative in their values. They seem to be so proud of doing it 'naturally,' as if my son is somehow 'unnatural.' One woman said, 'Oh I could never do that. All you are is an incubator for your husband and another woman's child.' Another said that I was immoral and unethical. The hard part is that they had a point and I wound up feeling so bad. But, this person's prejudice was inclusive of all IVF procedures. She asked, What do they do with the extras?

"When does life begin? I consider myself pro life, but I am not someone who will use violence to make a point. So, these things made me question whether I had been selfish in my desire for a child. The truth is, I am still struggling to make peace with this choice. I wish I could offer something to comfort others that are faced with the same choice. What I can say is that it is all worth it. I am so happy that I have my son. All of the debt, we are paycheck-to-paycheck people and had to do seconds on our seconds to have the means for these treatments, all of the heartache—it was so worth it. I am glad that I had to use a donor because otherwise the child conceived would not be my Juan. I'd rather have my Juan than any other child in the world."

Everytime I read her entry it brings tears to my eyes. She is so grateful for her son and understands that the other woman's contribution, her egg, actually helped to make the child she loves so dearly exactly who he is. That's a much healthier attitude than feeling in some way that she was slighted or merely an incubator, as the woman she mentioned so cruelly put it—simply because biologically it wasn't Maria's egg that contributed to her son's DNA.

"When it came to a choice between egg donor and adoption, it was easy," Maria explained. "I would not be able to go through a birth mom changing her mind. I was so emotionally fragile by this point it would have pushed me over the edge. I needed more control than that. Besides, I wanted to be pregnant. That part of the process was important to me. Wound up doing a high-risk pregnancy with preterm labor and preeclampsia and spent two months on strict bed rest. I even had birth complications (placenta acreta). Nothing about becoming a mom was easy for me, but I would do it again in a heartbeat. The love I feel for my son is indescribable. I do not know the identity of the donor but I think I have enough to go on that with help we can find her someday. I thought of doing it now but I am not quite ready. Maybe in a few years. I want my son to know how much love went into creating him.

"Before we chose the egg donor she wrote a letter to her potential offspring. This is what the letter said.

'You were conceived with love, giving, wanting and, I'm certain, painful perseverance on the part of your birth parents. Please realize how much you are valued. You were very wanted and are very special. Many people and much energy contributed to make a miracle—you!'

"What more do I need to feel good about this choice, I ask you? I am truly blessed."

Did We Really Win the Race?

There is an epilogue to overcoming a midlife infertility crisis. While the race against time is over, getting over it is something else. Although your beloved child is now in your arms, it took a long time for him to get here, time you could have spent moving forward with your life. But instead, because of things out of your control, you were hovering in limbo until destiny handed you your legacy. Even though we are divinely grateful for a child, once he is here there is a quiet resentment that it took so long. There isn't a week that goes by that I don't look at my youngest daughter and think, "And it took me three years to have you. If I would have just gotten pregnant sooner I could have had two more years with you." So by achieving motherhood at midlife did we truly win the race? I'm not sure you ever win a race against time. What I did learn from my infertility is that I no longer *wait* to do things I really want to do. And, I no longer take *anything* for granted.

FOUR

Nine Months and Counting

"No one told me how differently I would feel with this baby. You think you know yourself. Hell, I'm forty-one years old! I used to pride myself in my knowledge of who I was and how centered I had become over the years. Then I got pregnant. I cried all the time. Where does that come from? It's like this pregnant woman is in my body, crying, and I'm watching her, thinking. 'You are really silly. Why are you crying?' "

—SANDRA, A FIRST TIME MOM AT FORTY-ONE

Most midlife mothers are well informed about what physical changes to expect when pregnant, but it's the emotional and psychological considerations that take them by surprise. And it's not just the first-time midlife mother who finds herself in such a quandary. Women who have previously had children are often caught unaware by the uncertainty of their emotions. My first mistake was believing that since I had been through this before, I could predict how my body and mind would respond to once again being pregnant. I found, as have so many of my sisters, that each pregnancy is different—not only because physically each pregnancy is different, but because *we* are different with each pregnancy.

I was about seven weeks pregnant the first time my emotions took off and ran all by themselves. I was sitting at a stoplight listening to a song that I must have heard at least a hundred times. For some reason it hit me differently this time and there I sat, weeping in time to the music. An elderly woman pulled up next to me. "Are you all right?" she called through an open driver's side window. "Yes," I replied. "I'm just pregnant." She smiled a knowing smile and slowly pulled away when the light turned green. But I felt like an idiot. I was old enough to have control of this. What was happening to me?

Liz Beth, Liz to her friends, recounts a first-time midlife pregnancy experience.

"I thought women who cried at TV commercials were really stupid until I was ten weeks pregnant and overcome with emotion while watching something really corny on TV. My husband came home from work and there I sat in front of the TV crying like a baby. I felt so out of control. I just wasn't prepared for that aspect of the pregnancy."

Rest assured that crying easily and mood swings are both normal responses to the hormone changes of pregnancy. A good gauge as to how serious these mood swings will become is how sensitive you are each month before your period. If you suffer with PMS, you will most likely be equally sensitive while pregnant. These symptoms seem to ease a little in the second trimester, but will probably be back in full force once again in the third trimester. If you're really having a problem coping, it's best to mention it to your health care provider. Although antidepressants are very rarely prescribed to pregnant mothers, you may be a candidate.

The Wonder of It All

Like most who spend years trying to have a child, when I finally did become pregnant, I felt like this was the culmination of an acute religious experience and undeniably good luck. *It was different this time.* When I was younger I took getting pregnant for granted. As a matter of fact, getting pregnant was something I tried not to do. I got pregnant in a month my first time. In my mind, I knew there would be more children. I didn't know I would get a divorce and it would be ten years before I could again conceive. Pregnant again in my late thirties, the whole process seemed awesome to me. I was acutely aware of each change in my body, each movement the baby made, each subtlety that went by completely unnoticed years before. I bought the book *A Child Is Born*. Actually, I bought four copies! I had them all around the house. I read it every day. It was a great tool to help me talk to my other children about pregnancy and what was happening to the baby. All four copies were dog-eared and worn from use. Every time I looked at the book I felt as if I was visiting our little stranger. My husband was equally fascinated. We would lie in bed, look at the pictures, and figure out when our baby got his fingers and his toes, or if she was sucking her thumb.

"When I found out I was pregnant, I was floored." Mary Louise Pinkerton, a forty-five-year-old first-time mom, laughed. "I've never once had a pregnancy scare. I didn't believe I could have children. I've been married twice. One time for twelve years! Now I was in a relationship with a man who had just turned forty. It was more than casual, but we hadn't talked about 'till death do us part' either. I cannot even explain how I felt when the results came in. After I heard the news, in one split second my whole life's direction changed and I have never looked back."

Your first reaction to your pregnancy was probably excitement, but it may not be long before you start to question your rationality. "There was one day," Mary Louise continued, "when I was about four months pregnant, I really looked at myself in the mirror. I sort of pulled at the wrinkles around my eyes thinking. What was I doing? Do you know how old you are? But, then Jim walked in, sort of cuddled up behind me and looked into the mirror, too. He told me I looked beautiful, radiant, actually, and I thought, *Thank you, God, for this new chance. Thank you, God, for having enough faith in me to know that I can now be a good mother.* I'm not a particularly religious person, I just don't know what else to think. The whole thing—getting pregnant, getting married again, was such a bizarre thing. If this had happened even five years ago I wouldn't have been the mother I could be today. What a trip life can be."

If Ambivalence Rears Its Ugly Head

Not all pregnant midlife mothers share a sense of wonder and enthusiasm. Some take quite a while to feel positive about their pregnancy—if ever. Lots of pregnant midlifers have confessed that the desire to have a child came naturally, but pregnancy seemed like a huge mistake. Ambivalence loomed like a dark cloud, and it was difficult to break the cycle. To complicate the issue, newly pregnant midlife mothers coping with indifference feel guilty about their ambivalence. "I looked for the joy," a midlife mom confessed. "It just took me a while to find it."

No one knows why some of us rejoice in pregnancy while others regard it to be just one more obstacle to overcome. Shifting hormones and past personal experiences, which help to form our attitude about life, affect each of us differently. Realizing that every feeling is normal because we are each individuals may be a catalyst to relax and enjoy what is ahead.

I'm High Risk?: Medical Facts

When I had my last child, I was surprised when my doctor categorized me as *high risk.* "Why?" I asked him. "I feel great."

He explained that women over thirty-five might be regarded as "high risk" for a variety of reasons. First, age thirty-five is considered the cutoff date for a risk-free pregnancy because of the risks associated with having an amniocentesis. There is a chance for miscarriage associated with the test—statistically, 1 in 200—and that problems may arise as a result of the test itself. At age thirty-five, studies show the chances of having a child with a chromosomal abnormality are comparable to the risks associated with having an amnio. Therefore, doctors chose thirty-five as the cutoff date for a risk-free pregnancy because the risks of having a child with a chromosomal abnormality equaled the risks involved with having an amniocentesis. That was the original premise, but it may no longer hold true. Although the chance of a chromosomal abnormality has not changed, technicians have been performing amniocentesis for years, so the risks associated with the procedure are now significantly reduced.

Mothers at midlife are also considered "high risk" because as women get older they do not ovulate consistently. After forty there's a good chance that they may produce two eggs during one menstrual cycle or not ovulate at all. This explains both the reason why a midlife mother may take twice as long to become pregnant, and when she does, why there is a higher incident of twin births. Twins, or multiple births, as your doctor will refer to them, often translate to *high risk* from a medical point of view because your health care professional now has more things to worry about—you and two (*or more*) babies.

There was another reason my doctor categorized my pregnancy as high risk—something I had forgotten about completely. Although my first daughter was eight when I became pregnant, nine by the time the baby was born, she was in the footling breech position and delivered by cesarean section. In the past, one cesarean birth automatically meant another because it was feared that a previous cesarean might cause the uterus to rupture during subsequent labors. Because of a change in the way a c-section's incision is made, horizontally across the bottom of the uterus rather than vertically down the length of the uterus, there is now less of a chance of rupture. (I'll talk more about cesarean deliveries in the next chapter.)

Additional Dangers That Pertain to Midlife Mothers

Even though we feel great at "our age," there are some health concerns in addition to the ones already mentioned that midlife mothers need to take seriously when having children. Older mothers are more prone to gestational diabetes, preeclampsia (also known as toxemia or pregnancy-induced hypertension), and there is a higher incidence of cesarean section births.[*]

According to Dr. William Gilbert, professor and vice chair chief of the Division of Maternal-Fetal Medicine in the Department of Obstetrics and Gynecology at UC Davis, there are valid reasons for these concerns. Dr. Gilbert told me that as a woman ages, the elasticity of her blood vessels decreases, which can lead to an increase in blood pressure, or hypertension. This condition can then lead to an increase in preeclampsia and underlying kidney disease. In addition, a woman at midlife weighs more than when she was when she was younger, plus the added weight of pregnancy can put more stress on the "older" pancreas. Both of these conditions can lead to an increased frequency of diabetes during pregnancy.

And, the sixty-four thousand dollar question? Why is the rate of cesarean deliveries so much higher in midlife pregnancies? Dr. Gilbert seems to think that just as a twenty-four-year-old can usually run faster and jump higher than a forty-four-year-old, the cervix and uterus are no different. The cervix of an older woman may take longer to dilate, and the uterus of an older woman may be less efficient at contracting during labor. Dr. Gilbert also admits there may be

[*]Gilbert, "Pregnancy After 40," in *Journal of Obstetrics and Gynecology*, volume 93, January, 1999.

another logical explanation for the increase in c-sections in midlife mothers. Although immeasurable, patient and physician anxiety may be a contributing factor. "And, as the number of woman having their first child over forty increases, it is hoped that anxiety and the cesarean birth rate will decrease as a result."

To be consistent with statistics, it would be more likely that a woman would deliver vaginally if she had a child in her twenties, and have a cesarean delivery if she again became pregnant at midlife. Of course, I did it the other way around. Thirty-nine years old, with a previous cesarean, I had no trouble giving birth the good old-fashioned way.

GESTATIONAL DIABETES

If you don't think it could happen to you, just wait. I am living proof that as a woman ages, there is a higher rate of gestational diabetes. At twenty-nine, I sailed through my first pregnancy with no complications until that c-section extravaganza, but lo and behold, finally pregnant again at thirty-nine, feeling absolutely perfect, I was diagnosed with low-level gestational diabetes. I had no symptoms and no family history, and the diagnosis took me by complete surprise. "What does that mean?" I asked Mike, my ob/gyn. (I call my ob/gyn by his first name. To my reasoning, if he's seen me naked, we operate on a first-name basis.) "Is the baby okay?" He assured me the baby was fine, but being pregnant was putting a little strain on the way my pancreas regulates the level of sugar (glucose) in my blood. Because of the diabetes, the baby may be larger than predicted. I was told to watch my sugar intake, be very careful with fruit juices because they are high in sugars, and have absolutely no chocolate for the entire pregnancy. "Oh my," I said with a sigh, "I don't know if I can do that." "You have to," Dr. Mike told me. "If you don't, both you and the baby could get very sick." The last thing I wanted to do was put my baby in jeopardy, so I did not eat chocolate for the entire pregnancy. But the first thing I ate after the baby was born was See's chocolates. A box sat next to the birthing bed.

How Do You Feel When You Have Gestational Diabetes?

My diabetes was not severe so I felt nothing. I walked into my doctor's office after fasting and taking a glucose-tolerance test expecting to hear that everything was just fine. It wasn't, and from that point on my sugar intake was always on my mind.

Here is why gestational diabetes is so difficult to detect without the proper tests. Women who have diabetes during pregnancy report an increased desire to urinate, something that pregnant women have been complaining about since the beginning of time. They also report increased hunger; again, a common side effect of pregnancy. Dizziness is a symptom of gestational diabetes, but many pregnant women feel occasional dizziness. Other symptoms are blurred vision and weigh loss rather than weight gain. A blood test is the only sure way you will know if you are gestational diabetic.

Midlife Mom Memo:
Using Nutrasweet as a sugar substitute. With so many foods using chemical additives, it's not surprising that many of us automatically think that aspartame, better known as Nutrasweet, a sugar substitute often found in low-calorie foods, is not advisable during pregnancy. However, it's actually a type of amino acid, the substance all proteins are made of, and to date, research has not shown problems for a growing baby.

PREECLAMPSIA

Another possible complication for the pregnant midlife mother is preeclampsia. Also called toxemia or pregnancy-induced hypertension, it is more prevalent in first-time pregnancies and in "older" mothers. A diet too low in protein could increase your chances of developing preeclampsia. Most cases are mild and easily treated with bed rest and a regulation in diet. Symptoms are elevated blood pressure, a sudden weight gain, protein in your urine, but the symptom you will really notice is the swelling in your hands, feet, and perhaps your face. If you keep your prenatal appointments, your doctor is sure to catch preeclampsia and prescribe medication if need be, but if it goes untreated, it could be very serious, progressing into convulsions or even stroke.

"I didn't realize I had preelampsia until my feet got so big I couldn't fit them into my shoes and they had to cut off my wedding ring!" chortled Marla, a second-time mom at forty-four. "And, it took me by surprise because I had my first child at forty-two with absolutely no problems. I was expecting my second pregnancy to follow suit. It didn't."

Marla's ob/gyn prescribed medication to regulate her blood pressure and she was placed on a strict sodium-free diet for the remainder of her pregnancy. "But within days after my son's birth I no longer needed the medication," Marla explained. "And no high blood pressure since. I'm still a little surprised I had preeclampsia. I'm grateful my doctor caught it early."

MORE RISK NO LONGER MEANS HIGH RISK

The current consensus among those who know is that of course there are risks associated with having children at midlife, but they have been greatly reduced by recent advancements in medical science.

With consistent prenatal care *most* problems that arise during a midlife pregnancy can be met with a change in diet, exercise, or the introduction of a specific medication. Good prenatal care is the key. Choose your health care professional early into your pregnancy, don't miss prenatal appointments, and if complications do arise, report them to your health care professional immediately.

MULTIPLE BIRTHS

The National Center for Health Statistics tells us "the triplet rate rose nearly 400 percent for women in their thirties and exploded more than 1,000 percent for women in their forties." There are obvious reasons for these mind-blowing statistics, beginning with the fact that we are far more active than our sisters before us, and we actually consider having children as we approach forty and older. This was not the norm, even twenty years ago.

Next, with increased age comes the increased chance of infertility, and lots of us are taking fertility drugs or using IVF to help with conception. A frequent side effect of using fertility intervention is multiple births.

And last, the chances that a woman will have twins actually increases after she reaches thirty-five. This is attributed a higher level of gonadotropin, the hormone that begins the ovulation process. In older women, the gonadotropin level increases and she may produce two eggs during one menstrual cycle. Ethnic origin and family history also play a part.

Thanks to new reproductive technologies, our next midlife mother had triplets. Born in Israel, Rasmia is a registered nurse and a certified midwife. She has a thriving practice, The Natural Birthing Center, in Simi Valley, California.

"I have been married for thirteen years. My husband, Larry, was married before and has two adult children. It was always our plan to have children. Larry had his vasectomy reversed and we fooled around for a few years asking God, you know, but it was not in the plan. That's when I began IVF treatments, but IVF is very expensive and then you have to wait for a month in between. We tried IVF for ten years, five different times. The first three times it didn't work, I was disappointed, but I was fine, I got over it quickly. But, the fourth time, that was not good. You know, you have to wait for four weeks to see if it worked, and I was having the signs of pregnancy, breast tenderness, and nausea. I had my hopes up, but then the symptoms just stopped. I didn't want to believe it. I fought with the lab! I was devastated. And, I went through hell with the hormones that they give you to prepare for the in vitro fertilization. I was moody and angry, outraged, actually. The girls in the office didn't want to talk to me. I told everyone, don't disagree with me because I am not myself."

"PMS times ten?" I asked.

"PMS times a million. It was a terrible experience."

Rasmia continued. "Then Larry told me this would be the last time. He could not take it anymore. Because he had a vasectomy for ten years there were problems with the reversal, so each time we tried IVF they had to surgically remove Larry's sperm. He was exhausted."

"So it was an ordeal for both of you?"

"Yes, honey. It was very much an *ordeal*. They implanted four embryos, three took. God knew this would be the last time. Three different little personalities. Two boys and a girl. My doctor really wanted me to have an amnio, but when you are pregnant with triplets, it's not just one amnio, it's three. Three sacs means three amnios. After all I went through, I didn't want to risk it. Beside, why would I need an amnio? I wouldn't abort if there was something wrong. I had lots of faith. I sincerely believe that God only gives you what you can handle."

About twenty-four weeks into her pregnancy Rasmia was put on bed rest. "It was getting very hard to breathe. I couldn't walk up stairs, I would lose my breath. I said in a prayer, "You wanted me to have three babies. You gave me three babies, now don't take my breath." My doctor said the babies are growing quickly and I have too much amniotic fluid. They were up under my ribs and pushing on my lungs. He put me on bed rest and gave me medication to reduce the fluid, and then I felt much better."

Rasmia's plan was always to return to her practice after her babies were born. "My practice is very family oriented. We are in the business of birthing babies! I encourage my patients to bring their children to the office. Now they see my babies, too. I hired a nanny to help, and I will be a nursing mother, too, plus I work with another midwife, so we will split up the late-night calls."

I had to laugh. Not to be cruel, but I know how time-consuming it was to nurse one child. Although I loved it, and I would recommend breast-feeding to anyone, breast-feeding three babies? At once? It conjures up all sorts of laughable images, I must say, but Rasmia has it all figured out.

"Life is a challenge. Besides, how much do new babies do? You breast-feed them, you keep them clean, and they sleep, at least for the first few months. I have my nanny, the other midwife, my husband, and my sister is here for six months. How much help do I need?"

She was so convincing I found myself agreeing with her. "Well, what else do you need?"

"Listen," said Rasmia. "I have been taking care of human beings for twenty-three years. I know what I am in for. My job is very difficult. I already do not sleep through the night. My patients call me because of false labor. I have to meet them. I do it all because I love it, and because I love it, I don't feel it. It is the same with the babies.

"I am extremely happy. I walk by the babies' room every morning, I look in, and I think, 'There are my babies.' It gives me such excitement!"

To me, Rasmia is the personification of today's midlife mother.

She's confident, knowledgeable, loving, and grateful for life. She acknowledges that her experience makes her who she is, and with that experience comes the calm satisfaction that she can bring more to motherhood because of her time here on earth. She asked me to promise to stay in touch, and I thought, "Are you kidding? It is *my* pleasure."

MULTIFETAL PREGNANCY REDUCTION

With the increased number of women depending on medical science to be become pregnant, it is inevitable that some will be faced with the decision of whether or not to reduce the number of pregnancies they are carrying. This is called multifetal pregnancy reduction.

Multifetal pregnancy reduction is most commonly performed to decrease the chance of preterm delivery when a mother is pregnant with more than three viable fetuses. It is a particularly painful decision for those who have been fighting infertility, to become pregnant with so many babies that they simply are unable to carry them all to term.

A good friend who knew I was writing this book called me on the phone in tears. Her sister had been fighting infertility for years, and at thirty-nine, after four in vitro tries, she was finally pregnant, but with five babies. For her health and the health of the babies her infertility specialist was suggesting she reduce the fetuses to only two. The entire family was in an emotional uproar. No one knew what to do.

Assisted reproductive technology (ART) is a wonder, but as in the case of my friend's sister, it can be a double-edged sword. No one can tell you how to make such a decision. We can only support you in your choice.

Multifetal pregnancy reduction is usually done within the first trimester of pregnancy and is performed by a maternal-fetal medicine specialist. Such a technologist is available only a few centers around the country. These centers supply counseling to family members who need help in coping with making such a momentous decision.

If you have to face multifetal pregnancy reduction, don't try to cope with it alone. Reach out to the people around you, talk to your doctor, and get all the information you can to help you make an informed decision.

Coping with Weight Gain and Change in Body Image

Just watch TV or read a magazine for five minutes and you recognize that the media is still pushing youth and being thin as the key to Nirvana. So here we are, first at midlife, and second, pregnant and expanding our waistlines, once again walking against the tide of society.

If a woman's personal self-worth and sex appeal is somehow intertwined with her personal appearance, the weight gain associated with pregnancy can make her feel insecure and stripped of the authority her appearance once supplied. Although she may admit to being happy about the pregnancy, she may also secretly mourn the loss of what she sees as her claim to fame, and fear it won't return after the baby is born. This insecurity is only compounded in the woman who may be struggling with "aging." Is she intimidated by age or does she regard it as a medal of honor? Does age make her less appealing or more appealing? There are the lucky ones, the women for whom weight gain is not a concern, and they sail through pregnancy unscathed by social pressures. However, for most of us weight gain is a major pregnancy issue—midlife or otherwise.

"This isn't a beauty pageant," Lucy told me. She is a new mom who put off having a child until forty, then took two years to conceive. "I'm pregnant. Finally, I might add. I don't care what I look like. I care that my baby's healthy and that I'm healthy. In that order."

Of course we all agree with Lucy on an intellectual level, but after priding myself on my size 6 for ten years after the birth of my first daughter, I wasn't happy when my clothes began to get tight. Granted, I knew there was a little guy in there and I wasn't putting on weight for no reason, but being three months pregnant got to me. You don't look pregnant at three months; you just look overweight. It's not until four months when you start to develop that little belly that you have a visual excuse for all to see. To make matters worse, I was three months pregnant at my ten-year high school class reunion and here was my twenty-year class reunion coming up fast. I was three months pregnant . . . again! I went, a little reluctantly. I remember shaking my former classmates' hands. "Hi!" they said. "You look so, so . . . healthy!" "I'm pregnant," I just kept saying, over and over and over again. Many of them looked at me like I was nuts. Pregnant? At our age? One girl friend that I hadn't seen since graduation had a little too much to drink. "Did you have a boob job?" she asked. "I don't remember them being that big in high school." "They weren't," I replied. "I wasn't pregnant in high school." It got to the point that I just shook hands and said, "I'm pregnant!" all in the same breath. Finally, I blamed it on the clothes. "Nothing looks good on me right now." I really hate maternity clothes.

Samantha, a practicing attorney, was fed up with the styles available when she was pregnant with her son Alex. "All those little baby doll clothes they design for pregnant moms? That wouldn't do for the office. I had to concoct my own style. I bought lots of cotton knit clothing that expanded with me."

Me too, but I didn't want stretchy clothes. I had too many bumps and bulges I wanted to camouflage past the pregnancy bulge. When I couldn't zip my favorite jeans without seeing stars, I headed straight to the fabric store. I bought an eyelet gun and turned my jeans into lace-up jeans that fit through my sixth month. After that, those jeans with the stretchy panels in front started to look good to me. It just took me a while to get into the stretchy panel mind-set.

Those who study such things tells us that the average women should gain between twenty-five and thirty-five pounds. I've always envied those women who could actually do that. When, at four months I had already put on twenty-five pounds, my doctor freaked out. Not a clear-his-voice, raise-one-eyebrow doctor freak-out. A "No, no, no! This will never do!" freak-out. "I don't know what happened," I said, not taking responsibility for my actions. "I do," he snickered. "You're eating too much." The man went to how many years of college to figure that out? Then he tested me for gestational diabetes, it came out positive, and from the standpoint of food, the rest of my pregnancy got very boring.

Looking for someone who understood my plight I searched the Internet and decided to join an e-group for midlife mothers. That's where I met Paula. She lives about an hour away from me, but we often converse by E-mail. At the time of the following entry, she was near her time of delivery and counting the days. Paula had sent me entries from different times in her pregnancy. This one was noteworthy, not because it is particularly eloquent, but because it's how many of us feel toward the end of our pregnancy . . .

"I'm feeling big as a house and what shows up in my mailbox today? The Vicki's Secret Swimsuit catalogue! Waaaaaaaah! I want my body back. Okay, I'm not a toothpick like them at the best of times, but waaaaaaaah . . . I'm not a house! I just want to be able to wear normal clothes and bend over and pick up toys and hold my son on my lap, or even pick him up for that matter, and walk up the stairs without having to stop and rest every five minutes, and not have to get up 3–4 times in the middle of the night, and be on my feet for more than 15 minutes without feeling like my pelvis is going to split in two, and be able to turn over at night in less than 5 minutes and get in and out of my car without a major production, and not be eating half a bottle of Tums a day, and . . . Waaaaaaaaaaaaaaaaaah!"

Enough said.

Cravings

No one really knows why pregnant women have cravings, but it is suspected that it's the hormonal and emotional changes that occur during pregnancy that start us looking for strange food combinations. Cravings are only dangerous if you can't control them and if they work against you. For example, if you have high blood pressure and you crave salty foods, or if you are diabetic and you crave sugary foods. Both of these combinations can be dangerous for you and the baby. But in moderation, giving into cravings is a natural part of pregnancy.

Stats on such things tell us that the food craved most often by pregnant women is chocolate. Second, ice cream, and third, citrus fruits or juices. And I have to admit, during our conversations, quite a few midlife moms did confess to such cravings. "Having a craving for a particular food is so bizarre," contributed a midlife mom who was surprised by her initial cravings. "I've been on this earth for almost forty years. I have never craved a food. I thought cravings while pregnant was just an old wives' tale. Then I got pregnant and I have to have cheeseburgers, the greasier the better."

Another midlife mother admitted to craving cheeseburgers, but made specifically from deer meat, while still another had to have her cheeseburger from Wendy's, no place else. I craved wonton soup and spicy burritos from Taco Bell. Both loaded with sodium. Don't ask me why.

"I expected everything to go just as my last two pregnancies," admits Deanna Leona, a forty-year-old woman who is starting a second family with her new husband of fourteen months. "I had no cravings with my first or second child, but with this last one? I had to have sweet potatoes. Not yams. Sweet potatoes. And the sweet potatoes couldn't be microwaved; they had to be baked in the oven so the skin got nice and crispy, and then I drenched them with butter. Mashed it all up and ate them with a spoon like pudding. And, the funny thing is, I've made them like that since the baby's been born and they just don't taste the same."

"While I was pregnant I craved shrimp," explained Dory, a new mom over forty. "I'm a vegetarian and haven't eaten any animal product in over ten years, so for me this was pretty weird!"

Perhaps the strangest craving came from another midlife mother from Kansas who wrote via E-mail, "I will admit this to only you, and I will not give my name, but I craved coffee grounds straight out of the can." What can you say to that?

A pregnancy craving observation—pregnant mothers are extremely brand-aware. You can't just eat "yogurt." For one woman, it had to be Yoplait yogurt. "It's the consistency," Glenna observes.

"You can't just eat peanuts," Janice, another pregnant midlife mom revealed, for her, "They have to be Planters peanuts, because of the taste that is derived from their particular combination of oil and salt."

I had to have my burritos from Taco Bell. We, midlife moms? Well, we are one gourmet food-lovin' bunch.

Midlife Mom Memo:

My doctor told me that I was putting on weight too quickly. I knew the culprit. I craved ice cream, so I made up this substitute.

JANN'S BLUEBERRY FREEZE

2 cups frozen blueberries
(other fruits don't work as well as blueberries)
1 cup nonfat milk
Nutrasweet to taste

Pour the milk over blueberries and wait for 30 seconds until the milk gets kind of slushy.

Top with Nutrasweet to taste.

Mix it up and eat immediately before the milk melts again because then the blueberries taste flat.

The Truth About Sex During Pregnancy

In every book I have ever read about pregnancy, it mentioned women whose sex drive goes through the roof when they are pregnant. I've always wanted to meet such women because it never happened to me. I felt too bloated, too wobbly, too short. Yes, short—all that weight, I felt short and round. I'm not saying I didn't enjoy sex while pregnant, it's just every time I did, I would get a surge of Braxton-Hicks contractions and I thought I was taking the baby's life in my hands. Not until my doctor advised me that it was highly unlikely orgasm would prompt preterm labor did I relax. A lot. It's amazing how just a little bit of knowledge can change your entire attitude.

"I loved sex during my last pregnancy," admits Robin, an outspoken midlife mom of forty-two who we heard from in the last chapter. "It was the first time in my life I didn't have to worry about getting pregnant!"

And, Bonnie, who just called me with the news that she is again pregnant with number two at forty-three said, "Sex when I was pregnant was great. During the first trimester, even though I was tired, I still craved sex. Shortly after learning we were expecting, we went on our annual summer vacation (a very quaint place—island off the New England coast). It was like a second honeymoon! During the second trimester, I think my husband thought I was some sex-craved woman. Hubby has a very high libido, but mine was out of control! We continued to have sex at least five times a week until week 36, when doctor said no more because I was dilating and effacing."

If you don't feel like Robin and Bonnie, there's no cause for alarm. Perhaps you can find comfort in the fact that many of your pregnant midlife sisters have confessed to an almost nonexistent desire for sex. Aside from the fact that they feel unattractive because of their changing bodies and crazy mixed-up hormones, the fatigue that comes in the first trimester is often a turnoff. Plus, sex is always the first thing to go when a doctor detects trouble.

When at eight weeks pregnant it seemed I started my period right on time, my husband and I headed straight to the ob/gyn's office, but first I called him on the phone. "Mike," I said. "I'm coming in!" Just as concerned as I, he rearranged his schedule and saw me right away. I was given an ultrasound; he decided everything was just fine, and then proceeded to pour water on a paper towel to demonstrate that a little blood actually looks like a lot of blood. Analogies or not, it *was* a lot of blood to me and I was hyperventilating all the way home. Bed rest and, you guessed it, absolutely no sex, brought me back to health. By twelve weeks both the baby and I were just fine. My husband, on the other hand, had developed a strange nervous twitch.

Alexis, a forty-three-year-old mother of a two-year-old, pregnant with her second child, has a cute story about sex while pregnant. At the time of this writing, Alexis was days away from giving birth to her second son. When I asked Alexis about sex, she laughed. "I am so pregnant, I can't wait for this baby to get here. We went to bed last night—my husband and I were reading. He put his book down and was looking off into space and I asked him what he was thinking. He said he just wanted this baby to get here. Nine months was so long to wait for him! Well, what an opening! I wasn't going to pass it up. So, I said, 'You know, sperm has all kinds of good hormones in it that help soften the cervix and get labor going,' thinking he would jump at the chance. He starts poking me in the forehead with his finger. 'What are you doing?' I asked.

" 'Well,' says he, 'How would you like to get woken up by this?' *Poke, poke, poke* . . . 'He'll have brain damage!' "

This isn't just an amusing story; there are men who are actually afraid that they might hurt their unborn child if they have sex with their partner while pregnant. I can assure you it's a myth, both from personal experience and medical fact. If you're experiencing a normal pregnancy with no complications, it's perfectly safe to have sex. The baby is protected by your flesh and amniotic fluid and there's no way you can poke him or her in the head with anything, let alone your willy. But, they *can* hear in there . . .

Bonding with Your Unborn Child

Studies have proven that newborns respond to the familiar sound of their mother's voice or to the native language of their parents. Teddy bears are even implanted with devices that play the sound of the intrauterine heartbeat in order to calm fussy babies. Since it is commonly accepted that children can hear in utero, new mothers find themselves doing all sorts of things to assist in bonding with their unborn children. Some read to them. Others play music. Georgia, a new mother at forty who lives in the Sierra Nevada Mountains of Northern California, tells a sweet story of how her husband, Daniel, who is from Germany, sings to their unborn child. "Daniel used to sing Bridget, our first child, to sleep in my tummy with a German lullaby, and she loves that lullaby to this day. I have enjoyed and bonded much more with this baby in utero than I did with Bridget. I think that is because I know this is the last time I will be pregnant and I want to savor every minute."

Although my own mother has passed on, my mother-in-law is

still living and often visits me in my office while I'm writing. Her long-term memory is sharp as a tack, but because of a battle with a brain tumor, her short-term memory often fails her. Each time she visits my office she asks, "And, what book are you writing, now?" It's been the same book for the last two years, but when I tell her *Midlife Motherhood*, she beams, and again tells me the story of when she was pregnant with my husband.

Today, for some reason, she probed further. She was interested in the exact passage on which I was working. I explained I was writing about how mothers bond with their children before the children are born, and I asked her if she had any insight on the subject. "When you are young," she began, "I don't know if you worry about those things so much. I was eighteen when I had Larry, and twenty-one when I had Sharon. I had lots of time to be with them."

Lots of time. Perhaps that is why the topic of bonding so interested midlife mothers. Could it be that midlife mothers understand that time moves quickly and bonding with their child *before* it is born allows them more time to be close?

When it comes to bonding in utero, I had so much trouble getting pregnant that I was on a first-name basis with my daughter when she was still a zygote. I talked to her all the time, especially when I was in the car. I can only imagine what people thought when they saw me driving down the street chattering away to absolutely no one. But someone was there, right there with me, and I was thanking God every step of the way. My husband used to talk to her, too. One night, when he was being particularly silly, he laid his head right near my belly button and started calling her name. Each time he called something would bump, either a foot, or a hand, or an elbow. We never knew exactly what body part was responding to his calls, but my husband was convinced she could hear him. I just remember the first time he saw her he said, "So, you're the one who has been knocking? Let me introduce myself. I'm your daddy." Ironically, she looks exactly like him. Basically, Nature took his head and placed it on the body of a little girl.

My friend and midlife mother, Ginny Porter, didn't take to pregnancy with her second child quite as easily as she did with her first. She was always busy, with projects piled up one after another. As a matter of fact, Ginny and her business partner, Jack, a certified personal trainer, designed the exercise program featured in *Midlife Motherhood*. Ginny talked to me for quite a while about the mental preparation midlife mothers need to make so as to bond with their unborn child, especially if they have already bonded strongly with a first child.

"I was about six months pregnant and very busy," said Ginny. "I hadn't made the usual preparations for another child. I hadn't finished decorating my daughter's room. My mother took me aside. 'Ginny,' she said. 'You haven't bonded with this child yet.' No, I hadn't. She wasn't even born yet and my mother was concerned that I wasn't bonding. But, mothers are very perceptive. I think my mother could see how close I was to my son and knew how busy we were, she was saying, emotionally, 'Ginny, it's time to make a place for another.' Not instead, but, too. Of course nature has a way of making everything work together, and my daughter is incredible. But, I did have to slow down and change my mind-set so that I was ready for my daughter to be added to our family."

Your Second Time or Third Time or . . .

A mother for the second time while in her mid-forties, Darlene's story is not the typical one of the new mother at midlife. She did not wait to have children, nor was she surprised by an unexpected pregnancy. Darlene had been married to the same man for more than twenty years. She simply decided now was the time.

"Bruce and I were very content with our life. We own a building business. He's a general contractor, and I have always done the books. Our daughter, Jeanne, was happily away at college. Then one day, my best friend, Georgia, called me up and said, 'Don't laugh, but I'm pregnant.' Georgia is forty, remarried for the third time, and has a son, ten, and a daughter, six. I didn't laugh. On the contrary, I found myself green with envy. Jeanne, as a baby, flashed in my mind, and for a second I felt rejuvenated. I thought, Oh, how exciting. Georgia can start all over. She can share all that she knows about life with this child. I pictured the sweet chaos of having a toddler around the house, and then I thought, *I'm not too old. I'm only forty-three.*"

Over the next few months, Darlene's outlook on life slowly changed. "I started to notice babies again. While in the supermarket I cooed at unsuspecting infants. I talked to toddlers in the mall. I found myself surfing Web sites that sold baby apparel, and as I watched Georgia's belly grow bigger I decided, *Why not? I'll talk to Bruce and see what he thinks.*

"When I decided to initiate the conversation, Bruce was having a particularly rough day. The subcontractors scheduled to pour the foundation of a home did not show up and the entire job was at a standstill. He was frustrated and overwhelmed and when he sat down in his office the last thing he needed was his wife to start talking about babies, but I did it anyway. I said, 'Bruce, how do you feel about having another baby?' His face went blank, and then he fell forward and let his head hit his desk. I think that was the night I got pregnant."

I asked Darlene how Bruce felt about this sudden change in his wife of twenty-odd years. "I haven't been married to Bruce this long for nothing." Darlene smiled. "He is the most open, communicative man I know. Having another child was the farthest thing from his mind when I brought it up, but he loved our daughter and I think he, too, was looking for something else other than work to be the center of his life. We love each other very much but, well, Bruce was ready, too, I guess."

Darlene then explained that she was surprised how quickly she got pregnant. "I thought it was going to be difficult. You read about how it's more difficult to get pregnant as you get older, but it wasn't for me. It seemed like I got pregnant immediately. The next month I was on the phone with Jeanne breaking the news."

At first Darlene's daughter, Jeanne, thought her mother was kidding. "And, I thought she was nuts," Jeanne told me. "But as she spoke I could hear that she was happy. If Mom's happy, I'm happy."

"And, that's when the morning sickness started." Darlene laughed. "Right after I hung up the phone. If I had bought stock in a soda cracker factory I would be a millionaire by now."

Morning sickness took Darlene by surprise. "I never had a tinge of nausea when I was pregnant with Jeanne. I ate anything I wanted. I put on twenty-seven pounds. I lost twenty-nine pounds by the time Jeanne was six months old. I was thin and healthy like that for over two decades. Everything went as planned. This pregnancy was just the opposite! I retained water like crazy. I was very tired all the time, and I blew up like a balloon. I didn't get gestational diabetes, though. I was fine in that department. I remember reading somewhere that you put on sixteen to twenty pounds by the time you weigh the baby, the placenta, the water gain, the increased weight of your breasts, so the day after I have the baby I got on the scale expecting to drop twenty pounds and feelin' great about it. I lost eight pounds. Joshua weighed seven pounds, seven ounces."

As Darlene had already mentioned there were definite physical differences in her two pregnancies, but I was more interested in her thoughts comparing the two pregnancies; how she felt about having this baby in her forties compared to having her daughter in her early twenties. "I knew this was going to be my last child," Darlene explained. "So I treasured every minute of the pregnancy, especially after the baby started moving. I remember when Jeanne moved the first time, I giggled. When Joshua moved the first time I screamed, 'He moved!' I really let it register.

"One of Bruce's best friends is a fine wood cabinetmaker and he made us a beautiful rocking chair to put in the baby's room. I would sit in the chair and rock back and forth even before Josh was born. I read to him in the middle of the night when there was no one else awake. I relished my time alone with him, sending him secret messages that told him how much he was loved and how much he was wanted. When he was finally born, I knew him. And, he knew me, because I held him in my heart for months before he was here."

I knew exactly what Darlene meant. It wasn't that I didn't appreciate being pregnant in my twenties. It was just that I took so much for granted in my twenties—especially my health. Life takes on a whole new meaning at midlife, and therefore this pregnancy took on a whole new meaning. I was so excited that I could do this again at a time when I understood its importance. My daughter wasn't the only one who was born on her birthday. It was definitely a rebirth for me, too.

Impatient Toward the End . . .

Yes, we are, and age has nothing to do with it. Not only do you feel huge, but also by the time you are ready to deliver it's really time to get on with your life. Nine months, forty weeks . . . all right, already.

"I know exactly how they feel," a midlife mom told me in confidence. "I am a week overdue now and it's starting to depress the hell out of me. I don't know what's wrong with this child. This has never happened to me before. A friend of mine who is also pregnant is having painful early contractions. She complains constantly, but I would gladly take them from her!! I would love to have a cramp, a pain, *anything*! Is that sick or what? I'm actually asking for pain!"

The truth is, very few women actually deliver on their due date. First babies are often late, and it's not uncommon for second or third babies to be born before the actual due date. Nearly 10 percent of all babies are *post-term*, or born after forty-two weeks.

Even if your baby isn't late, praying for labor to begin is understandable. The last month you put on weight more rapidly than before, you retain more water than in the first few months, and your ability to move around is severely hampered by your swollen belly. The thought of getting back into "real" clothes seems like a dream too good to be true. And, trying to recount everything you learned in childbirth class, you count the days, no, the hours, until you feel that first little twinge of labor that signals it's time for the big event.

FIVE

The Big Event

"I didn't go to childbirth classes for my second child. Now that I look back on it, I'm not sure why. I had a c-section when having my first. My water broke almost a month early, and I was rushed to the hospital holding a sign in the window of my car announcing that I was going to have a baby, and please move out of the way. When I did arrive at the hospital, it was determined the baby was in a footling breech position. My doctor said it was c-section time, and a few hours later I had a bouncing baby girl.

"So, when it was time to have my second daughter, I had no idea what labor or childbirth felt like. I wasn't afraid. I figured labor couldn't be any worse than the menstrual cramps I had endured over the years. (My life changed when I discovered 800 milligrams of ibuprofen taken at the appropriate moment.) The cramps miraculously disappeared and therefore I thought medical science would help me sail through this delivery. I had a very supportive husband, a doctor I trusted. I was ready to be pregnant. And when it was time, I was ready to have the baby."

—JANN BLACKSTONE-FORD, MIDLIFE MOTHER AT THIRTY-NINE

There's more to the story. My husband thinks he's a childbirth veteran. He had two kids from a previous marriage, the last one six years ago, so he felt he was fully competent to coach me through a birth without a childbirth class refresher course. Believing just about everything he says to be true, we just cruised up to the time I went into labor, thinking we had this under control.

According to my doctor's calculations, my daughter was well on her way to being a ten-pound baby, so everyone was watching me very carefully because of that previous c-section—except my husband, the childbirth veteran, who decided to celebrate at the local sports bar with his buddies the evening we knew I was going to go into labor. I called him to make sure he was well within the legal alcohol limit—which he was, and told him to come home now because my contractions were five minutes apart. He didn't believe me. Being that he was a childbirth veteran, his experience told him that if my contractions were five minutes apart, "I would be screaming." I tried to explain to him that his ex-wife, with whom I am very good friends, mind you, may have been a little louder when her contractions were five minutes apart, but I was just fine. It was time to come home. He did, and we were off and running to the hospital.

When we arrived my doctor checked and found that I was dilated only two centimeters. Both he and my husband, two men who have never personally given birth, very smugly told me that there was no way I was going to have this baby until around eleven the next morning. It was 10 P.M. Both of them suggested I go home. I could stay if I liked, but it would be a very long wait. I knew it wasn't going to take twelve hours, I was the one having the baby, so I stayed, but the doctor went home.

No surprise to me, six hours later I was ready to give birth. The doctor comes scurrying in from his drive from home, surprised that I had progressed so quickly. He looked at me sort of bewildered, as if to say, "How did you know?" "Call it women's intuition," I said out loud.

I had already set up the video camera a couple of hours before. I was adamant about taking the video from *my* point of view so I could actually show the tape to my friends. My husband, the childbirth veteran, was so nervous he forgot how to turn the camera on. He's fumbling. I'm having contractions.

"You're supposed to help me breathe," I say huffing and puffing all by myself. He still can't figure out how to turn on the video camera. I have another contraction. He's still fiddling with the camera.

"Honey," he finally says in desperation. "I'm sorry, but I can't figure this thing out."

He hands me the camera. I have a contraction, turn it on, and hand him back the camera. Then I have another contraction. He starts to film. He's standing next to my head using the angle I mentioned before.

For some reason my leg won't stay in the proper position. The doctor is sitting on his little stool down there, remember, and I see him trying to hold my leg while performing an episiotomy. This concerns me. Then he yells, "Larry!" That's my husband. "Hold her leg!" So Larry quickly tucks the camera under his left arm and takes off to the other end, evidently still filming while attempting to hold my leg. If you tilt your head to the right you get a pretty good view of my daughter being born . . . at 3:58 in the morning, from the wrong end. Actually, it was the right end, just not the end from which I wanted to film. It was 3:58 A.M. *not* 11:00 A.M. What do men know?

There's an epilogue to this story. About nine in the morning my husband goes home to get our other children so they can see the baby and visit mommy. Their ages at the time were ten, nine, and six. My husband then proceeds to fall asleep on the couch in the birthing room and lets me baby-sit. Four kids. Five hours after I gave birth. *He* was tired.

This chapter, parts written a little tongue-in-cheek, will cover the various aspects of labor and delivery so you can be prepared for what is in store. Truth be told, you can get most of the medical information you need about labor and delivery from the zillions of pregnancy books already published. *Midlife Motherhood* will examine how the older mother feels about her labor and delivery experience and what she would like to pass on to you, another midlife mother.

Childbirth Classes

I'm starting this chapter with a discussion on childbirth classes, as I know how much they can help prepare both you and your partner for labor and delivery. Women who take childbirth classes are known to feel more positive about the birth experience and need less medication than women who have not taken classes. Had I known then what I do now, I would have insisted on a refresher course—even enough to touch base with a knowledgeable instructor and maybe take a tour of the hospital. For me, knowledge is power and I would have been far more centered as I gave birth if I had a weekly touchstone where I could have asked questions, confided in other pregnant mothers, and let my husband commiserate with other partners.

There are a variety of natural childbirth methods taught in childbirth classes, all developed to lessen the anxiety of the mother and to decrease the need for drugs to ease pain during the labor and delivery process.

The three most common natural childbirth methods are the Grant Dick-Read method, the Lamaze method, and the Bradley method.

The Grant Dick-Read method is the oldest. In his book *Childbirth Without Fear*, published in 1944, Dr. Grant Dick-Read explained that he felt educating mothers about childbirth reduced fear, which in turn reduced their muscular tension and resulted in less pain during labor. He was also one of the first to advocate educating fathers and allowing them into the labor room.

Shortly after Dr. Dick-Read's teaching began, French obstetrician

Ferdinand Lamaze's work began to spread and through the years has become the most widely used method for natural childbirth. The Lamaze method is a little different in theory than the Dick-Read method in that it emphasizes relaxation during labor by distracting the mother from the pain of labor by using concentration and specific breathing techniques to ensure that labor contractions are productive.

The Bradley method was developed by Dr. Robert Bradley in 1965 and described in his book *Husband Coached Childbirth*. This method highlights the help of a partner to coach the mother through her labor and delivery. Instead of using distraction and patterned breathing as in the Lamaze method, the Bradley method stresses inward focus and slow abdominal breathing to help the mother "tune-in" to her body's natural flow during the birthing process. Special emphasis is put on nutrition and avoidance of drugs during pregnancy, childbirth, and breast-feeding.

Childbirth courses not only cover various methods of childbirth but also offer other benefits. They discuss the various types of deliveries, alternative pain relief during labor, and hospital procedures.

Childbirth Class Content Should Include Information on:

* The normal progression of labor and delivery.

* Specific ways to promote the natural progression of labor and delivery.

* Natural pain management.

* Medications commonly given in labor, such as drugs to relieve pain or advance labor.

* Common medical interventions.

* When is a cesarean section performed?

Childbirth classes fill up early. Check with your health care professional to see where and when he or she suggests you register. Most professionals suggest you complete your childbirth courses before your thirty-sixth week of pregnancy. This is because *most* babies can be safely delivered after this date and if you do happen to go into early labor, you will be properly educated and prepared for what is ahead.

Questions to ask Your Childbirth Instructor

* What is her general philosophy on childbirth? Does it match yours?

* How does she feel about the use of drugs to ease the pain of labor?

Some childbirth instructors hold very strong views against the use of painkillers during labor and these strong opinions may increase a new mother's anxiety if she is unsure of what is ahead. Discuss this at length with your instructor.

* How many couples are in a class? Ideally, there should be no more than ten couples in a class (that's twenty people).

Too many couples means your instructor may be spread too thin and not give you the attention you need.

* Before you sign up, ask if you can sit in on one class to see if you like the instructor's approach.

If you don't like the instructor's approach, check to see if the facility has another instructor's class you can attend.

When you're in labor, you'll pick and choose from the skills that you learned in class. You will quickly discover which ones work for you and which ones do not.

Are Labor and Delivery Different for the Mother at Midlife?

Labor may be longer for a woman at midlife simply because her older uterus may be less efficient at contracting than a younger mother's during the labor and delivery process. Postpartum bleeding may last a little longer, too, for the same reason. The definitive word here is *may*. Each labor is unique. Because your first delivery was quick and painless does not guarantee your second delivery will be the same. You will not know how your body will react until you enter labor. This may make you a little uncomfortable. The most important thing to remember is to relax, have faith. Even if you don't realize it you have a fabulous support group—yourself, your body, Nature, your doctor or birth attendant, and your partner.

Is It Time?

Since medical science still cannot pinpoint what brings on labor, it's not surprising to hear mothers wonder, "Is it time? Am I really in labor?" We have so many bumps and kicks and twinges while pregnant, it's difficult to distinguish if one of those twinges is truly the onset. Even mothers who have had a slew of kids still question labor's onset. Is this the real thing, or isn't it?

There are some definite signs when you are entering labor and the following list is meant to make it easier for you to determine *if it's time*. Let me caution you, though. Some of these signs are quite subtle and you may not know when they happen. Except for the last one—you'll definitely know when that occurs.

* Braxton Hicks contractions become stronger and more frequent.

* Lightening, or the baby drops to a lower position in the pelvis. You may notice it is now easier to breathe.

* Engagement, or the baby's head lowers in the pelvis and rests against your cervix.

* Cervical effacement—your cervix thins and becomes shorter.

* Loss of mucus plug.

* Rupture of membranes (your "water breaks").

Julie was a nurse and so she figured she would know when she was in labor. She laughed as she told me the story of the birth of her first child when she was thirty-eight. "Here I am, as big as a house, and two weeks late, when I start to get these cramps that I just knew had to be labor. Never mind the chicken fajita I devoured two hours before, I was in pain and calling the doctor. He told me to come right in, so I called my husband at work, he zoomed home, and we were off to the hospital. My husband was running stoplights and I was sweating the pain was so bad. I was a little confused because the contractions did not let up. There was just this constant pain, and that had me concerned. I shifted my weight a little to get more comfortable, and passed some very loud gas. The pain left immediately. It wasn't even false labor—and I have never lived it down."

False labor is difficult to diagnose. Some first-time mothers are confused by painful Braxton Hicks contractions in their third trimester and believe they are in labor. No one's laughing at you if you are on your way to the hospital as soon as you feel them. If you don't know what you are looking for, it's difficult to distinguish between Braxton Hicks, false labor, and the real thing.

"I experienced false labor," explained Elaine. "And, now that I know what labor feels like I can say false labor didn't really compare, but I can see why some women are confused." Elaine went to the hospital four times thinking she was in labor. "The main difference in the labor contractions were that with real labor the contractions came from my entire uterus and from my back, whereas the false labor started at the bottom of my uterus and never traveled any farther. Then, after about two hours, the contractions just stopped. Four different times. It was very frustrating."

Here is a quick checklist to see if your labor is the real thing. If you are confused, never be afraid to discuss this with your health care professionals. Call them! Tell them your symptoms and follow their instructions to the letter.

TRUE LABOR	FALSE LABOR
Contractions are at regular intervals. For example, you have a contraction consistently every 5 minutes.	**Contractions are at irregular intervals.** For example, you have your first contraction, another 10 minutes later, another 30 minutes later . . .
The time between contractions *decreases* with time.	**The time between contractions remains irregular.**
Contractions get more intense with time.	**Contractions do not grow stronger or stop.**

TRUE LABOR	FALSE LABOR
You feel the contractions consistently in your lower abdomen and/or back.	Contractions are in a variety of areas.
Changing your position does not affect contraction frequency or intensity.	Changing your position stops the contractions.
Your cervix begins effacement (thinning) and dilation.	There is no change in your cervix.

If you have never had a child, any nagging pain you have in the vicinity of your abdomen is considered potential labor, but there are some preliminary signs that alert you that labor is coming—like your water breaking. Listen to Martha's story.

"I wasn't due to have my daughter for three more weeks. I hadn't even begun my maternity leave. I got off work early and decided to go shopping for a few last-minute items. I wanted a pretty flannel nightgown, not a grandma one, to wear for the delivery and so I headed alone to the mall. My eventual destination was Nordstrom's, but there was a shortcut through Sears'. As I walked through the sock department I heard what I thought was a child's balloon pop, and it startled me. I became more startled when I realized that the sound was not a balloon popping, but my water had broken and it was gushing all over the floor.

"That's when I became frightened. I had read in all my pregnancy books that labor begins after your water breaks, so I had this image of the pain becoming excruciating in between the argyles and the tube socks. There I stood, cellular in hand, trying to figure out who I should call first, my husband or my doctor, with water gushing everywhere. My doctor won. And, by the way, labor didn't begin until late that evening."

Fear of Labor

Fear of the unknown plays a huge part in a woman's attitude toward labor and delivery, and for some reason, women at midlife seem to believe they should be more prepared than their younger sisters. Perhaps it's because we believe that we have been around for quite a while and should understand the labor and delivery process. Anyone who has had a child, however, will tell you that there is nothing more humbling than being in labor. Try to find comfort in the following information. First, you don't have control over what kind of labor you will have. Second, you cannot predict how long or how painful your labor will be.

The best way to combat fear is education. Learning why there is pain associated with labor may help to decrease your anxiety. Very simply, it is the dilation of your cervix while the uterus contracts to push the baby out that causes pain. It helped me to visualize my uterus contracting during labor. I knew each contraction brought my daughter closer to being born, and that's what I concentrated on.

Here is a personal story to demonstrate how the fear of pain associated with labor can affect your judgment. Remember I explained that the doctor told me upon entering the hospital that I wouldn't have my child until eleven the next day. I took him for his word. At three-thirty in the morning the pain was intense and I told my husband that I could not endure this level of pain for seven and a half more hours. He asked the doctor to give me some pain medication, Stadol, which the doctor did without checking how far I had progressed in dilation. Then the doctor checked and realized that I was dilated to 8.5. The reason I was in such pain was because my cervix had dilated from 4 centimeters to 8.5 centimeters in 45 minutes, but I didn't know what to expect. I wasn't sure how intense the pain would get. After I received the medication I had trouble breathing and my doctor administered a drug, Narcan, to counteract the pain medication. A little stoned, but fully aware, I had my daughter twenty minutes later. I have the sideways videotape to prove it.

Pain Medication

You may be able to tell from the tone of my story that I was disappointed that pain medication was administered. A product of the sixties and seventies, I am of the school that if you can do it naturally, you do. I watched my sister give birth to four beautiful daughters with no pain medication, so I knew it was possible. In my case, I think pain medication was administered due to a combination of things—my fear and ignorance of the pain associated with labor, and the doctor's anxiety.

Like me, many women feel a letdown when they use pain medication during labor. Some feel they were deprived of the full labor experience, while others fear that the baby will be harmed if medication is used. I remember still feeling the affects of the medication after the birth and being afraid to nurse my daughter for fear it would affect her in some way. The attending nurse assured me that no harm would come to her, so I relaxed, but I have learned since that my fears about pain medication and its effect on my child were not unfounded. When pain medication is administered too close to delivery it may severely lower your blood pressure and cross the placenta to slow the baby's breathing. Make your decision as to whether you will use pain medication depending on the intensity of your pain after consulting with your doctor.

Most Common Types of Pain Relief Administered During Labor
Ask your doctor about the following medications:

* Demerol

* Sublimaze

* Stadol

* Nubain

These are all relatives of morphine, a narcotic, and can be given to the mother every two to four hours. It definitely takes the edge off, but too much medication can really make you loopy. I am very susceptible to any sort of drug. My doctor gave me the same amount he would have given any woman of my age and weight, but it was way too much for me. Although I have lovely memories of the birth of my child, they are laced with memories of being given too much pain medication.

* Epidural

An epidural is the most popular form of pain relief during labor and must be administered by an anesthesiologist. A catheter is inserted into your lower back into the space above the membrane covering the spinal cord. The catheter stays in place throughout labor. Medication is then sent through the catheter to numb the nerves going to the uterus, vagina, and perineum. You remain conscious, but feel no pain. There may be a drawback to an epidural, however. Since you have no sensation in the lower part of your body, pushing during delivery becomes less effective and you may need the help of forceps or a vacuum to aid you in the birth of your baby.

Alternatives to Pain Medication

Some women do not want to use medication to relieve the pain of labor and defer to alternatives like alternating their position during labor, breathing techniques they learned in childbirth class, massage, or hypnotherapy.

Although I have been trained to use hypnotherapy for dental pain, and my hypnotherapist did use hypnotherapy to control pain during her labors, I was a chicken. I know the success of hypnotherapy lies within you and the power of your mind, and since I wasn't specifically trained to use this method for childbirth, I didn't trust myself. Looking back, that was just the fear of the unknown talking. Knowing how well hypnotherapy works for overcoming pain during a dental procedure, for me it would have been an excellent choice to overcome the pain of labor. I would suggest this method to anyone who does not want to rely on drugs to control pain during labor. You might want to check out a great book on the subject called *Hypnosis for a Joyful Pregnancy and Pain-Free Labor and Delivery*, by Winifred Conkling and Nancy Barwick.

Your Labor Coach

A labor coach is someone you choose to assist you through labor. This person attends childbirth classes with you and learns how to help you make the birth of your child a positive experience. The coach is there to hold your hand, get you ice chips if you're thirsty, help you stay centered during contractions. The truth is, your body does what it is supposed to do during the birthing process. You can control the pain through various methods, and if there are medical complications you should look to your health care professional to intercede. Your labor coach is there for emotional support. He or she is your personal cheerleader.

YOUR PARTNER'S INVOLVEMENT

Being pregnant together can teach you a lot about your partner. Although he or she may have had children previously, it may not have been with you. Even if you have had children together, since labor and deliveries can be different, their reaction to the delivery may be different. My husband, usually a take-charge-kind-of-guy in normal life, couldn't figure out how to turn on the video camera he was so nervous. But when it came to getting down there and breathing with me to calm my fears, he held my hand and made those goofy he-he-he sounds with the best of them.

Two months ago, Delia, a web designer, had her first child at forty-two. Her husband, Jack, was there by her side. "Jack is fifty years old and has never had kids. He wanted to do this; I think he viewed it as his last chance to be a father. He's a little squeamish, and he left the room during the videos of various types of deliveries during our childbirth classes. I really wanted him there with me during the birth, but I was secretly afraid he couldn't take it. He was a trooper, though. My labor progressed normally and he was great. I will never forget some of the wonderful things he whispered to help me keep my focus. So loving, so sensitive. The birth truly brought out another side of Jack that I thought was there, but had never really seen. It's a time I will treasure on many levels."

THE SINGLE MIDLIFE MOTHER

Society is no longer surprised if a single woman at midlife decides to have a child. Some do not choose to marry, some are not involved with the child's father, and some simply decide that now is the right time and opt for artificial insemination. This may make finding someone to support you through the labor and delivery a little more difficult, but certainly not impossible. Friends and extended family are excellent choices. If they will not consent to help you, ask your doctor for suggestions. Professional labor coaches are available. Doulas of North America, an organization of women who help new mothers, may help you contact them. Contact information for this group is listed in the resource guide in the back of this book.

A few single midlife moms told me that they found their labor coach at their childbirth class. They befriended other single mothers and bonded with *their* coaches, thereby making new lifelong friends.

Delivery

Have you noticed that everyone has a birth story? And, each one is more painful than the next? And when you are pregnant, everyone wants to tell you their very painful, unsurmountable-odds-while-having-this-baby story? It's like they came out of the woodwork as I waddled around, and as I got bigger and bigger and more obviously pregnant, more women wanted to tell me their stories. It got to the point that before anyone started, I prefaced it with a question. "Is this a nice birth story?" If they started to make a face before they spoke, I asked them to hold that thought for a few more months. I did not want to sabotage my thinking with negative thoughts. I like to hear the funny stories or the sentimental stories—the stories that make you laugh or bring tears of joy to your eyes. I wanted a diversion, to be inspired, not frightened, and I wanted time to slow down, so I could savor every minute.

"Before I had my first child, I did not think of myself as a particularly strong person," explained Rachel, a first-time mom at forty. "I'm an artist and I believed that along with my artistic abilities came emotional instability. I never felt particularly in control when under stress. As a matter of fact, the day I found out I was pregnant I made an appointment with a counselor. I'm embarrassed to say, I just didn't think I was strong enough to handle the birth. I had seen births in movies and on TV, and I just knew I could never do that. But, when it came down to it, I did. Labor lasted just under twelve hours. It progressed normally, and for the first time in my life I felt like I was actually in control. The experience changed me, and not a moment too soon. My son has a mother who is a much more secure woman than I was before he was born."

The best way to understand delivery is to listen to other mothers' birth stories. Since your body is going to do exactly what it wants to do during labor, to hear about other successful, trouble-free births may be the most encouraging thing you can do. We'll start with Loris' story. She was forty-three when her daughter Pearl was born.

A First-Time-Birth Story

Labor started innocently enough. Her husband left for work as usual at 7 A.M. His last words to her were something like, "Gee, honey, maybe I should stay home today. You might go into labor."

" 'Ha, ha,' I said," chortled Loris. " 'It'll be days.' And, I went back to sleep. At 8:30 A.M. I woke up to go to the bathroom and as I stepped gingerly away from the bed my water broke. It was a slow trickle, but I knew it had broken all the same and I started to freak out a little bit. Can't lie. I was frightened. I was alone and I wasn't sure what to do. Fluid running down my legs I'm walking around the house, trying to find my *What to Expect When You're Expecting* book, just to make sure I'm really in labor. I find the section that describes when your water breaks. I fit all the criteria, but I'm still not sure, so I call my uncle who just happens to be a retired ob/gyn. 'Yes, honey,' he says, 'call the doctor and call your husband.' I called my husband and told him to come home, and I drive to the doctor's office, dripping all the way. (I had put some clothes on . . .) My doctor said to go directly to the hospital, my membranes had ruptured. I guess he read the same book I did.

"I get back in the car and head off to the hospital. My husband meets me there along with Mom, who decided at the last minute that she wanted to be present for the birth. I have a big argument with the doctor about using Pitocin, but he wins because I am a weenie at this point.

"At first it didn't seem so bad, but by 2 P.M. I am hanging off the bed, yelling, 'Oh God, make it STOP!' and I'm only dilated 4 centimeters. They tried a narcotic injection, but all it did was make me stupid . . . it didn't help the pain much at all. Accepting my pain threshold was on the negative scale, I opted for an epidural. Thank you; there is a God . . . what a relief . . . I could feel every contraction but they weren't very painful. In two hours I was ready to push. Pushed for thirty-five minutes, and, of course, the doctor thought I needed an episiotomy but, at that point, who was I to argue? The next push, out she flew, screaming at the top of her lungs! WOW! What a miracle . . ."

What a miracle! That's what we all say, no matter what our age.

Midlife Mom Memo:

Pitocin, also known as Oxytocin, is a drug used to augment labor if your contractions are not progressing well. It is administered through an IV, the amount increased slowly until your contractions are adequate. It was previously believed that the use of Oxytocin made contractions stronger and more painful, but we know now that this is not true. Oxytocin mimics the hormone that your body naturally releases during labor and simply helps things along.

Do You Need an Episiotomy?

When the baby is about to be born his or her head stretches the skin around the vagina. As the baby's head comes through, it may tear the tissues, sometimes dramatically, and an episiotomy, or an incision between the vagina and the anus, is performed. This is done for a couple of reasons. First, if the tissues are bound to tear, it's easier for your doctor to repair a carefully made incision rather than ripped skin. Second, if the baby's head is large, of course an incision to make the birth opening larger will ensure an easier presentation.

Not all mothers need an episiotomy. Although they are most commonly performed on women having their first child, some mothers are adamantly against having one. There are ways to get around it, massaging the perineum is a good example, but you will never really know if an episiotomy is needed until the birth attendant sees the size of your baby's head and makes the judgment call. Women who have had a previous episiotomy are often reluctant to have another. The incision requires stitches and they can itch and be very uncomfortable as they heal. Personally, I remember the pain associated with the episiotomy more than I remember the pain associated with labor. It's best to discuss all this with your doctor beforehand so he or she knows your feelings about having one performed.

Involving Your Children in the Delivery

Many midlife mothers have children spanning generations. Nancy, a forty-four-year-old midlife mother, and her husband, Bill, have had four children. "My daughter was my labor coach," Nancy volunteered. "She's twenty years old and had never seen a birth and was really into the process. This was my fourth child. My husband had been through it before. He said he was grateful Annie wanted to do it."

It was an easy decision for Nancy and Bill, but more difficult if the children are small. Children under four may not be able to understand what is happening and seeing Mommy in pain can easily scare them. Even if your child is ten or twelve and feels that they can handle it, it may be too much for them when it's time for the baby to be born. Lorraine, a midlife mom starting her second family after a divorce from her first husband, explained that her daughter, who was twelve at the time, was overcome with fear when she saw her mother's doctor perform an episiotomy. If you choose to have your children in the delivery room with you, make sure they are fully aware of what to expect. Have them attend childbirth classes with you to prepare. Always let them leave the birthing room whenever they desire.

We heard from a midlife mother named Eileen in Chapter 2. Her son was born with Klinefelter syndrome. During our initial conversation Eileen explained that one of the reasons she chose to have an amniocentesis was because her other children wanted to be present for the birth. Before she would consent, she wanted to make sure the baby was healthy.

All these things must be taken into consideration before you allow your children into the delivery room. Not understanding the birthing process, and seeing their mother in pain, could affect children for the rest of their life and color their own attitude toward any future births of their own. Eileen was very wise to take all the necessary precautions. As it was, five of her seven children were present at the birth of their youngest brother.

Cesarean-Section Deliveries

According to recent studies, almost half of all first-time midlife mothers give birth via cesarean section, and doctors do not agree on the reason why. We did hear a little about cesareans from Dr. Gilbert in the last chapter, but his comments only reinforce that there is no definitive reason why older mothers have more cesarean births. For this book, I was more interested in how we midlife mothers *feel* about giving birth in this manner rather than why. Although mothers don't replay frame-by-frame each aspect of a cesarean birth as they do with vaginal births, the feelings associated with cesarean births went from elation, "Yahoo! I hate pain!" to feelings of complete failure as a woman.

Lara, a forty-one-year-old second-time mom, gave birth to her first son by cesarean section, and this caused her a great amount of anxiety anticipating the birth of her second child. She explained that she had been diagnosed with endometriosis in her late teens and she had been treated like a hypochondriac for many years. She considered herself to have zero pain tolerance. "I just thought I was a wimp," she winced.

"With my first son's birth, I intellectually knew that a healthy baby was the most important thing, but it felt like I had failed as a woman to not deliver him. I just so badly wanted that experience to be picture perfect." What supplied a turnaround for Lara was the remark made by a nurse/midwife while discussing her past ob history. The midwife learned that Lara had a cesarean birth after thirty-seven hours of labor. Her son weighed 10 pounds 9 ounces! "Well," said the midwife, "I can certainly see why you would need to have a C-section. That was a *big* baby!" Somehow, hearing a midwife, who Lara equated with a low-to-no-medical-intervention policy, say it was okay to have a cesarean section made the last grain of self-doubt disappear.

She now looks forward to the birth of her next child with no reservations. "But," Lara concludes, "it took the maturity at midlife and self-education, learning that the male-dominated medical community isn't always right when it comes to women and their complex physiological and intellectual structures to finally relax."

I was surprised by the fact that some mothers felt that having a cesarean birth in some way reflected on them personally. When I had a cesarean, I have to admit, I was shocked when I needed one, but I didn't feel it reflected on me as a woman. Quite frankly, my oldest daughter has always had a mind of her own. She's the one with the magenta hair in our family. I am not surprised she was upside down and backwards in the womb. It's her. She's unconventional and a little contrary, and now that I know her better, a cesarean is completely consistent with her personality. Lara's comments prompted me to think more closely about my own daughter's cesarean birth, and I have to laugh. All these years I regarded her cesarean birth as her choice, not mine.

Cesarean Births: My Unscientific Study Results

I know statistics point to a high rate of cesareans performed on midlife mothers, but my personal calculations yielded much less than the statistics quote. If the stats are consistent with reality, out of the two-hundred-plus women I spoke to while writing this book, almost half would have had their children via cesarean section. I asked each and every one, women from all around the world, women I met personally, via the Internet or phone, and this group's rate was closer to 30 percent. There are some things I should note. I did not ask them to clarify if this was their first birth. I did not ask them to clarify if they had a previous cesarean. I simply asked if they had a cesarean birth or a vaginal birth, and roughly sixty out of the two hundred commented "cesarean."

I mention this because some midlife mothers expressed a fear of having a cesarean birth. This weighed heavily on their mind as they progressed through pregnancy. Just remember, statistics, numbers, can be manipulated many different ways, and the numbers depend on things like the control group, who was polled, where they live, their exact age (are they thirty-five or forty-five?). If you are healthy and have confidence in yourself, your birthing coach, and your medical attendant, everything will be just fine, even if you have a cesarean.

When This Is Not Your First Baby

Just as we accept that each pregnancy is different, mothers say the same thing about labor and delivery. Although you think you can anticipate what will happen when you give birth, no two births are alike. However, our thoughts and feelings don't really change from birth to birth. Our unbridled anticipation, frustration if things don't move fast enough, and then ultimately the love we feel for our child are with us each time.

My two births were very different. The first was a C-section, the second a vaginal delivery. I have experienced both worlds, and I wouldn't change a thing because it allows me to relate to both types of deliveries when other mothers discuss the birth of their babies. There were positive aspects to both deliveries. With the cesarean, there was no pain. With the vaginal birth, the recuperative period was *much* shorter. Looking back on them both, the thing that has stayed with me was not the births of my children, per se, but how miraculous is the human body and the labor and delivery process. Even though I had already had a child, labor and delivery was new to me. You live in this body for thirty or forty years thinking that you have control over it. Then you go into labor, Nature takes over completely, and you realize this is all bigger than you.

For those who have children ten or even twenty years apart, you may have forgotten the wonder of it all. I did. It is almost as if I have had two lives, the opportunity to keep living over and over. When I finally did become pregnant again, it was nine years after my first child was born, and I forgot what it felt like to be pregnant. I forgot how it felt to feel a baby move inside of you. I forgot the anticipation, the worry, and the elation. I thought, *Oh boy, I get to do this again*, thinking in the back of my mind that if there was anything I truly missed the first time, this time I would be sure to take note. And I did. This time I kept a journal. This time I took pictures. This time I paid attention.

Caroline Walden is a forty-five-year-old American who currently lives in the Czech Republic. Although she taught English as a second language to middle and high school students plus coached the tennis team when she became pregnant, she is now a stay-at-home mom.

Caroline and her husband, Serge, had two sons, ages seventeen and fourteen. She and Serge thought their family was complete, but a few years ago while debating whether or not to donate the crib and baby things to charity, Caroline mentioned that she wouldn't mind having another baby. Serge scoffed and said, "You just want something to do!" But, at age forty-four, Caroline found herself pregnant by "accident."

"We'd just been using withdrawal for the past few years, thinking that our reduced fertility would outweigh the risks. Lo and behold, there was no reduced fertility! Serge was shocked, but the more we talked about it, the more we warmed to the idea and started looking forward to the new addition. Serge was also afraid of birth defects, but I assured him that I was equally afraid and would have an amnio-centesis to rule out certain things. I went to the doctor and saw a heartbeat on the ultrasound. We were on our way.

"The pregnancy was uneventful. My ob/gyn, who never consid-ered me 'at risk,' said I was in fact doing a lot better than some women half my age, who had problems with sugar, weight gain, or high blood pressure. I think I enjoyed the pregnancy much more than when I was younger. I loved watching the baby move—everything just seemed so special and precious. I took nothing for granted.

"It was five days past my due date and the doctor, growing nervous, suggested an induction over the weekend. I'd been having a low backache all day Saturday. Serge and I got to the hospital at 7 P.M. Saturday night as scheduled for the induction. My ob/gyn met us, checked me into my room, and strapped me to a fetal monitor. When she came back after a half hour or so, she looked at the printout and said, 'Caroline, you're having contractions, about five minutes apart!' That was news to me—all I felt was the backache! She said maybe we wouldn't need the prostaglandin—that real labor may already be starting. She checked me internally—only 1½ cm dilated—no change from Tuesday. She wanted to wait for another half hour to see what would happen. We did, but there was still no change, except the nurse told her I had lost the mucus plug. So she decided to administer the prostaglandin suppository into the vagina. As originally planned, this was just supposed to get things ready for the main part of the induction on Sunday morning. But on me, wow, it worked. I could really feel the contractions now. When the doctor came back at 10:30 P.M. to check me internally again, she said, 'Wow, perfect! 5 cm! Let's go to the delivery room!' I walked with her and a nurse, Serge trailing behind, stopping about four times for contractions. By the time I lay down on the delivery table, I was 8 cm dilated! Serge sat behind me, still in his street clothes, holding my hand. (He gets queasy at the drop of a hat and said he didn't want to watch the actual delivery, but things were so intense and I had a death grip on his hand, and I think now he's proud he stuck it out!).

"The doctor said, 'Okay, Caroline I'm going to break the bag of waters—it can go very fast now!' Indeed things really did start moving. I pushed a couple of times. Somehow in the rush I was also hooked up to an IV ('just in case' the doctor said, and, in answer to my question, said there was just fructose in there for now). Finally, I think she said she'd put a bit of Oxytocin in the drip to make the contractions stronger. I asked to be on my side for comfort, and the doctor just said okay, but to tell her when I felt the urge to push. That felt like only seconds later—an unbearable pressure—and I said, 'It's pushing, it's pushing!' I turned over, and started pushing. I couldn't quite get through that big push, though, so somewhere in there the doctor gave me an episiotomy, which I didn't feel at all.

"Anyway, Katerina ('Katya' as we call her) slid out, crying as soon as she emerged, at exactly 11 P.M. I could see her in the doctor's arms. 'She's big!' gasped the doctor. Indeed, she weighed 8 pounds 14 ounces and she was 21½ inches long! The pediatrician checked her out, wiped her off, pronounced her just fine, all parts intact, and, as my doctor stitched me up, handed her to Serge, who sang her a Russian lullaby until he could place her across my stomach. It was beautiful; she was beautiful; we are ecstatic!"

After the Birth

After your baby has been delivered there will be a great sense of relief, but it's not over yet. A few minutes after the birth, the placenta, or afterbirth, is delivered. This stage of the delivery lasts anywhere from five to fifteen minutes. You may still have contractions, although they will be less intense. When the placenta separates and reaches the vagina, you may be asked to push once more. Many mothers, exhausted and preoccupied with their new little baby, do not even remember the presentation of the placenta. I don't remember, but my children do. As they waited outside the delivery room to see the new baby and me, my doctor came around the corner carrying my placenta in a stainless-steel bowl. Evidently it was a perfect specimen, and himself being fascinated, proceeded to show my children. It was a little much for them. My middle daughter, who was nine at the time, became afraid that something had happened to me and was as white as a ghost when she walked into my room. She checked to see if I was okay, looked at the baby for a second, and then walked into the bathroom and got sick. My kids still talk about that to this day.

To close this chapter on a positive note, here's one more story contributed by a midlife couple, Jeanne and Brian Cornelius. Jeanne was thirty-eight when her last child was born. Brian was forty.

After three daughters, Jeanne and Brian thought their family was complete, but Brian always wanted a son, so he convinced Jeanne to try one last time. Even though their daughters were ten, eight, and six, Jeanne consented and quickly became pregnant. Because Jeanne was at midlife, she decided to have an amniocentesis to make sure the baby was healthy. It took three weeks to get the results, and the day the letter came in the mail it was a big day for the Cornelius family. Brian broke out the video camera as Jeanne sat at the kitchen table, the three girls surrounding her, ready to open the letter. Brian zoomed in on Jeanne's face, waiting in great anticipation as Jeanne opened the letter. She quickly read it, and then looked into the camera. "Turn it off," she said. "Turn it off, Bri." Jeanne was pregnant with another girl.

Although Jeanne and Brian were extremely grateful that their little girl was healthy, Brian secretly hoped the test results were wrong and it really was a little boy hiding out in there. When Jeanne went into labor, intellectually he knew he was going to have a daughter, but emotionally he still had hope. He brought flowers for the mother, a stuffed Beanie Baby for his new little girl, and a baseball glove, just in case.

The labor and delivery went on without a hitch. Fourth baby, two-hour labor. When the afterbirth was presented, Brian was still hoping. He pulled the baseball glove from his back pocket. "Wait," he said to the doctor. "Maybe that's a boy." I know this to be true because I was there. You see, Brian is my brother-in-law.

Initially, we all prefer that our new baby be one sex or the other. At times that preference shifts back and forth—yesterday I wanted a boy, but today I think a girl would be nice. Some parents can only picture themselves with a child of one particular sex, only to be completely rattled when the opposite one shows up. Boy or girl, neither comes with an instruction manual, and that moment of transformation when you walk through your front door as a family for the first time is no more life-altering if you are holding a baby boy or a baby girl in your arms. Either way, life will never be the same.

SIX

Finding the New Normal— Getting Adjusted and Dealing with Change

"At forty-seven my husband and I adopted a child thinking that adding an infant to our hectic but rewarding life would be 'a piece of cake.' I now realize that this was really just a pipe dream I made up in my head to appease my ever-ticking biological clock. My daughter, Lucy, now two years old, is a live wire, to say the least, and this midlife mom is feeling the strain. I find myself wondering if life will ever get back to normal, and during a conversation with my best friend I expressed my concern. 'Jane,' she said. 'If it hasn't returned to normal in two years, it's time to change your perspective.' And, I realized she was right. I guess I just have to find the new normal."

—JANE CONNELLY, FIRST-TIME MOTHER AT FORTY-SEVEN

Finding the New Normal

After two years Jane was still waiting for things to return to the way they were before her daughter was born. With each new stage of her daughter's development, she held to the fact that life would once again regain its balance if she was just patient. Lots of midlife moms find themselves in the same predicament—waiting for things to get back to the way they were before children. It doesn't happen. From the emotional ups and downs caused by teetering hormone levels, to sleep deprivation, to the obvious adjustments that must be made when first becoming a family, *everyone* takes on new roles and finding *the new normal* may not be as easy as we once anticipated.

Moving from Me to Mommy

Most new midlife moms look forward to leaving behind their old lives, their past me-centered existence. As Lisa, a new mother in her late thirties, put it, "For so many years I was preoccupied with my weight, my attire, my career. Having a child and worrying about someone else was a wonderful relief. I was bored with me."

"I was bored with me." I loved it when Lisa said that. I remember laughing out loud at what I thought was the brilliance of her statement because it so perfectly put into words what many midlife moms had told me. They said they were ready for this and they wholeheartedly accepted the inevitable changes a child brought. Moving from me to Mommy was a welcomed transition. It was exactly what they wanted and they were excited about what life now had in store.

"Nothing was better than those first few months after we brought the baby home," one midlife mom reminisced. "Life was no longer predictable. Everything was new and I was alive. Really alive, again."

Everyday Reality

And then everyday reality sets in and life may not seem as euphoric as you first thought. Your mother or sister goes back home, your friends stop bringing over dinners "just to help out," and there's just you, your partner, and this little guy who takes up far more time and energy than you ever imagined. Granted, you love 'em to pieces and his or her mere existence brings out things in you that you only dreamed were there, but there's that ebb and flow to adjustment for the midlife mom that's sometimes hard to handle.

"When you've had one child, you think you know what you're doing when the next one comes along," explained Marni, a midlife mother we met in Chapter 1. "Then the next child turns out to be a completely different person requiring a completely different approach. As a result, with the third, you are humble. You don't have the swagger you had after mastering the first, but the wiser you believes you must have amassed a range of skills that will serve you well with number three. Then number three shows up and presents you with something really new: colic.

"I had thought that the powers that be would grant this ambivalent, if not reluctant, aging mother a child who was impossible not to fall madly in love with—an easygoing baby, a charming baby, a portable baby—like my other two. Wrong. She was the classic colic case, screaming for hours on end, every day for her first four months. When Nina was several weeks old, I signed up for a Mom and Baby aerobic fitness class. Mothers would situate their infants on blankets and quilts on the floor, and then dance around them for an hour to pleasant, well-modulated pop tunes. The babies loved watching their mommies jump and lunge and twirl; they cooed and burbled, cycled their chubby limbs, dropped off to sleep. All except my baby, who would be purple and shrieking. She screamed relentlessly, even as I held and stroked her while trying to do at least some of the leg movements. The other mothers were first-timers, and some of them would look at me like, 'Don't you know how to take care of a baby?' I thought to myself, 'I used to be like you. One day you will have a baby like this one, and then you'll remember me.'"

Many mothers love the infancy stage; others don't, and feel guilty about it. I found it quite comforting to hear from both sides because that's how I felt—sometimes I was elated, sometimes exhausted. I don't understand why society seeks to cubbyhole us into one category or another—if you adjust to motherhood easily you are a "good" mother. If you find the adjustment a little difficult, then there's obviously something wrong with *you*. Not so. Life has its ups and downs, therefore motherhood, a unique aspect of life, must have its ups and downs, too. The key is to trust your instincts. Listen to your own heart and inner voice and don't be swayed by what you are told you should think or feel.

In the beginning, I was so ecstatic about *finally* having a child that no amount of adjustment was going to squelch my enthusiasm. The first months were perfect, until exhaustion set in, and then I wasn't equipped to take care of the baby, my family, and prepare to go back to work. I looked to my husband for some help, but he's the kind of guy that hits the pillow and then you don't hear from him until about five-thirty the next morning. A baby crying in the middle of the night would never stir him. Knowing this, everything was on my shoulders, and after about three months of not sleeping through the night and trying to handle it all, I was exhausted and on the edge. The day I took my daughter to the doctor's for her DPT vaccination just about did me in. After the shot, she cried at the top of her lungs for three straight hours. Not a whimpering cry, but a squealing painful cry that etched its way into my psyche. Of course, the fear that *my* little daughter was the one in thousands that would have a reaction to the vaccination shot through my brain. As I waltzed around my bedroom holding her to my breast, softly singing every song I could think of to calm her, I felt as if I was in a dream. Things moved in slow motion. I needed a break. Most of all, I needed sleep.

Coping with Fatigue and Lack of Sleep

While some new mothers complain of being tired after a baby is born, midlife mothers complain of being exhausted. Bone tired. Now-that-the-baby's-asleep-don't-make-me-move tired. I even remember a time soon after my youngest daughter was born when I was just too tired to hide the Easter eggs for the older kids. The baby was born in early March and by the time Easter rolled around I was just three weeks into my juggling act. I lay down next to the youngest older child to tell him a bedtime story, only to wake up at two in the morning to the whimpering cry of a hungry infant. I fed the baby and then realized I hadn't hid the Easter eggs nor assembled the Easter baskets. Ten years ago this would have never happened. I delighted in special occasions. I would have lovingly gazed at my husband sleeping so soundly and quietly tiptoed around the house looking for innovative hiding places. This time I set the kids' shoes next to the Easter baskets and hid eggs in each one. That was fast and easy, and then I plodded off to bed.

We've all heard experts suggest, "nap when the child is napping," but I could never figure out how to do that. I'd close my eyes for one second and either my husband or a friend would call to find out how the new baby was. Babies are not conditioned to answer the phone when they hear it ring. I am, and each time it rang, I just lay there thinking, *Please let me sleep. I haven't slept in a year.* In my desperation, I decided to unplug the phone. You may wonder why it took so long for me to figure that one out. I am of the mind that if you don't teach a baby to sleep with a little home noise distraction, you are going to raise a very fussy baby. In my effort to desensitize my baby to family noises, I didn't take the proper precautions for my own well-being. Unplugging the phone made all the difference in the world. With an extra two or three hours of sleep a day, I started to feel more like myself. The little trials of my life ceased to flow into each other. They became separate little problems and I could address each one with new resolve. Best of all, my memory improved. I could actually find my car keys.

A great solution to getting a little extra sleep comes by way of an experienced midlife mom. "The best thing you can do is find a young neighbor girl, about ten years old, to help you with the baby. Ten-year-old girls love babies and they will sit and coo with them for hours. My next-door neighbor's daughter was wonderful. She was too young to be left alone with the baby, but she was old enough to keep an eye on her when I needed a little time to myself. And when I was too crabby to deal with anyone else, she miraculously understood that I was just getting used to being a mommy."

Coping with Hormones Gone Haywire

The older I get the more I understand the impact hormones have on not only my body but also my mental state. I have often reflected on how just a small amount of a chemical substance can alter the way we feel. Look at the size of a birth control pill, for example. Smaller than a pencil eraser, it's hard to believe that the amount of estrogen it contains can change your entire body chemistry and prevent something as monumental as ovulation, but that's exactly what it does. With this in mind, it's not difficult to understand that while a body is trying to regain its balance after having a child, you may experience a few emotional ups and downs.

Midlife Mother Alert:
The Baby Blues and Postpartum Depression

For some of us, however, a few emotional ups and downs does not really describe how we are feeling. Research tells us that almost 80 percent of all women having children will experience some level of depression after a baby is born, so after you and the baby settle in, if you find that you are plagued with feelings of vague sadness, uncertainty, maybe disappointment and ambivalence—you have thoughts like, "I wanted this baby for so long, why am I not ecstatic about it?" and you cry at the drop of a hat, you are most likely suffering from the baby blues. The onset of the baby blues seems to coincide with the time milk production starts and then slowly diminishes in intensity in two or three weeks after the baby is born. Although these symptoms are uncomfortable and may slow down your adjustment period, there is no cause for immediate concern. They will eventually disappear.

Midlife Mom Memo:

Adoptive mothers beware! The emotional adjustments that must be made when you adopt a child are not necessarily triggered by biology. Even though you are excited about the baby, a feeling of ambivalence has alarmed many adoptive mothers after the baby arrives. For some of us, that motherly bond is immediate, but for others, it takes time.

Postpartum depression, on the other hand, is something completely different. Although many think that the baby blues and PPD are similar and even use the term *postpartum depression* as a catchall to refer to feeling a little blue after a child is born, that's where the similarity ends. A far less common ailment that only 10 to 15 percent of all new mothers go on to develop, postpartum depression is not simply mood swings caused by hormone fluctuations. PPD is a *combination* of psychological, emotional, *and* physiological changes brought on after the birth of a child, and if not properly diagnosed and treated can develop into a debilitating illness. Although hormones seem to be the most obvious cause of PPD, things like sleep deprivation, medical complications in the mother or the baby, colicky babies, no support from friends or family members, and, perhaps, a history of depression or anxiety, also seem to contribute to the onset. Not enough research has been done on the illness, so the *exact* cause is still unknown.

Although Gwen, a new mother in her early forties, was never diagnosed with postpartum depression, the following comments are typical of the frustration one feels when suffering with it. After we spoke, I suggested that she see a specialist—not because she said anything that we all haven't felt in our lifetime, but because after giving birth her feelings of frustration and being overwhelmed could certainly be signs of PPD. Listen to what she has to say about her life after having a baby.

"Today, my husband got up right before I was ready to leave, about nine, as he had this job to do in Portland. I had already spent two hours with my daughter, watched Teletubbies and got her breakfast. When I asked him to dress her so that I could finish getting ready, he said he didn't have time and had to get ready himself. I am the one who gets her ready in the morning, takes her to day care and picks her up. He said he couldn't pick her up today because the car seat will take too much time, and he would work on it over the weekend. I am ready to get a divorce! I am so sick of men not doing the 50-50 thing. I spoke to a woman at work today and she said that men are just that way no matter what age they are. I went home to see how the pool plumbing was going a little while ago, and hubby just had to tell me I backed out onto the lawn this morning (we have a garage that is on the side). That was it! I yelled out to him as I walked back to my car, 'I am doing the best I can doing everything. If you want things perfect, you can take Angelina to school or let me hire a nanny!' This is the same old story I went through with my first husband. I really feel like a single parent. My husband and I never even have sex anymore. This is not what I expected when I got remarried at forty-two. I should have had my tubes tied."

Knowing what I know now, I realize that I was a perfect candidate for postpartum depression. Like Gwen, I felt as if I wasn't getting any help. My older kids were at the age when they really needed my care. I was stressed about returning to work. My husband is a builder and we were right in the middle of a building recession. My mother-in-law was ill and it was my responsibility to also help with her. Take those things, *plus* the hormonal changes after you give birth, and that's the recipe for postpartum depression.

It is important to note that the baby blues and postpartum depression do not necessarily affect you in the same way after each birth. I did have a severe case of the baby blues after having my first child. The reason I hesitate to call it PPD is because it went away, thank goodness, in about a month, but I remembered the feeling so well that when I did become pregnant again I asked my husband to watch for the warning signs, and if needed, help me alert a physician. (New mothers may not recognize their symptoms as PPD-related, and they may need prompting from a loved one to seek help.) After my second child was born, I did have symptoms again, but this time they were more physiological than psychological in nature. Because the symptoms were more tangible, they did not seem overwhelming to me. Plus, I knew what it was, and just that knowledge helped me to cope.

COMMON PPD WARNING SIGNS

First, your symptoms are real and do not mean you are weird or have anything wrong with you.

* Feelings of extreme anxiety or panic

* Feelings of inadequacy

* Thoughts of hurting the baby or yourself

* Frightening thoughts or fantasies

* Loss of control and feeling completely overwhelmed

The degree of intensity of these feelings can fluctuate, and at times seem more intense than others. If the symptoms seem to come and go, that does not necessarily mean that you are over the hurdle.

If you are concerned that you are suffering with PPD, seek help from a doctor or therapist who is experienced in working with women who have suffered from it. This is very important because although you love your family doctor, he or she may not pick up that the symptoms you are reporting as PPD related, especially if you are visiting your primary physician rather than your ob/gyn and it's been a few months since you have had your baby.

Midlife Mom Memo:

Jane Honikman, M.S., is the Founder of Postpartum Support International, an organization dedicated to increasing the knowledge, understanding, and social support for women suffering with depression brought on by the birth of a child. She suggests that your sleep patterns may serve as a barometer to help diagnose the blues and PPD. If you monitor your sleep patterns after you give birth and you can't sleep when your child sleeps, or you have trouble returning to sleep and sleep in general becomes a problem, further evaluation may be warranted. "This may be a signal that more is going on beyond the baby blues or normal adjustment to a new baby."

Most important, don't let the fear of being ostracized for frightening thoughts or fantasies stop you from seeking help. Doctors sometimes prescribe antidepressant medication for these symptoms, but medication alone is not the answer. If you do choose to take medication, experts recommend that you also seek help through counseling.

WARNING: We now know that the women who battle PMS and PPD also have trouble with menopause. They are just very sensitive to the hormonal changes in their bodies. The good news is, in the majority of cases, the symptoms of the blues and even PPD disappear with time, but for some it is a long road. The key? Don't be afraid to seek help.

WARNING: Doctors have not found a definitive reason as to why, but there are more cases of PPD reported by women who have given birth by cesarean section. The speculation is that depression is associated with any form of surgery, and a woman who has given birth via cesarean section is coping with the emotional and physiological upheaval of both major surgery and giving birth. That's a lot to have on your plate, plus as we have already mentioned in a previous chapter, midlife mothers have a higher incidence of cesarean births, so if you have had a C-section, be on the lookout for the symptoms of PPD.

Coping with the Less Obvious Changes

Until now we have concentrated on dealing with the things that are expected when adding a child to your life—lack of sleep, shifting hormones, PPD, but there's much more going on in the life of a new midlife mom that merits discussion. In our effort to regain our emotional balance after the addition of a child, we new mothers must face changes to all the primary relationships in our lives—the new relationship with our child, our own personal outlook on life, and the relationship with our partner are all affected in some way after the baby arrives.

Bonding with Your Child

Rumor has it that the first time you hold your child the two of you will experience an unexplainable immediate connection. Biological or adopted, you look into each other's eyes, Nature will snap her fingers, and you will both fall instantly in love with each other. Sometimes this does occur, but don't be disappointed if it doesn't happen like that for you. I can't say I felt an immediate connection when they handed me my youngest daughter. She didn't feel like an alien, someone from another planet, but I don't remember harp music, either. There are those stories where the clouds open, angels begin to sing, and it is apparent that this illustrious child must be yours, but there are also those stories of complete bewilderment and frustration. These are the feelings we don't often hear about, and they may seem even more intense to a new mother who has waited until midlife to have a child and is desperately seeking that perfect relationship.

Bonding isn't miraculous. It's not magic. It's an evolving human process, and there are lots of different ways to help you feel close to your newborn child. Breast-feeding is an excellent example. You are close to each other and only you are supplying the necessary nutrients to keep your baby healthy. But, if you don't breast-feed, are you a bad mother? That's how one midlife mother felt when she realized breast-feeding was not for her. She told me she felt her anxiety over her inability to breast-feed interfered with the bonding process. It probably did, but only in *her* mind. Bonding, by definition, means binding together *over time*. It's not necessarily an immediate process, and if you have a sense of ambivalence when you first hold your child, relax. Spend time with your baby. Hold your baby. Talk to your baby. Build a relationship with your baby and that feeling of closeness, or bonding, will soon come.

The Need to Reconnect with One's Self

I took my first breath when my daughter was about four months old, at least that's the first breath I remember after her birth. She was healthy, she occasionally slept through the night, I was on the other side of my postpartum whatever it was, and I finally realized what was missing. My privacy. I had none. I was *never* alone.

When I was younger, in college, privacy was not such a valuable commodity. I lived by myself, at times with a roommate, and when we needed privacy, we went to our rooms and closed the door. To me, a closed door means you want to be alone—but not when you have children. When your children are very young, you leave all the doors open so you can hear them when you are not in the same room. As they get older, it doesn't matter if the door is closed or not—they are right there, all the time. Nothing is private. Even if you lock the door, somehow they figure out how to break in, or they pound on the door and make you feel like a bad mommy if you don't open it right away. Not even going to the bathroom is a private affair. If someone in the family isn't going to the bathroom, they are talking about it. Bring a child home, and privacy is a thing of the past.

"When the baby was born, we finished off a room in the basement for my older son (who was then sixteen), and the baby got his vacated room," says Darcie Johnston, managing editor of my first publisher, Magination Press, the children's self-help imprint of the American Psychological Association. "We just barely fit. There was not an inch of free space. The males all used the basement for their work and studying. There was no place to put things. Every room looked like a storage facility, with stuff everywhere, cramped and cluttered.

"I am a writer, a musician, an artist. All my life I have had space to myself and stayed up late at night—writing, playing music, composing songs, drawing, painting. But now there was not an inch of space in the house that I could call my own, nowhere to go to have the peace to think, much less create.

"I can't say that after four years it has gotten better. I have just sort of shut down. I feel mindless. To keep my sanity I have had to go numb. But the prospects are changing. My younger son goes off to college in the fall. I have my eye on his room. I covet the space, the door. I know what color I will paint the walls, what furniture I will put in there, and how it will be arranged. I fantasize about it every day. My husband has seen me staring into space. It unnerves him. What I am doing is staring at my desk and my work supplies, visualizing them all in new surroundings, but he doesn't know that. He has no idea what this means to me."

I understand Darcie's lament. I used to have a room to myself. Granted it was a walk-in closet, but space is precious at our house and I converted the closet into an office. I had my computer desk set up in there, a file cabinet, and some drawers for sundry items. I had electricity brought in and I even had a phone line. I was so happy. No one ever bothered me in my closet. It measured six feet by eight feet. There was no room for anyone else but me! It was my private place and I could close the door and write to my heart's content.

Then my mother-in-law became ill and we decided that I should move my office into the spare bedroom so I could be with her during the day while she was recuperating. My new office became Grand Central Station. Kids in and out. The dog's new hangout. One day, I took a break while working toward a deadline to return to my husband doing the computer banking on my office computer. He forgot to save my document before he started.

My privacy, the privacy I took for granted in my lovely little hole-in-the-wall had vanished. Needless to say, I was not happy about this new turn of events. I had come to depend on my own space—a place, even a closet, where I could sit and compose my thoughts, close out the noise of the house, and work on my *own* projects. With that space gone, I felt disoriented and boy was I crabby.

But, all was not lost. Like Darcie, I came to realize that life would someday regain its balance and I would again have my own space. It would just take time . . . and a new password that no one in the house knows but me.

Tips to Reconnect With Yourself After a Child Comes into Your Life

* **BEGIN BY TRUSTING YOURSELF.** Take note of your positive qualities and *truly* rejoice in your personal strength. Give yourself the credit you deserve.

* **MAKE SURE YOU GET PROPER NUTRITION.** Losing weight is important to new mothers, but not at the expense of your physical and mental health. You have lots of time to lose the weight. Don't go on crash diets after the baby is born.

* **SET ASIDE TIME TO DO SOMETHING YOU LIKE THAT WILL LIFT YOUR SPIRITS.** Even if it is only a half hour to read a magazine, do some stretching, meditate, watch a funny TV show, or take a relaxing bath.

* **GET PLENTY OF REST.**

* **NURTURE EMOTIONAL SUPPORT.** Reach out past your immediate family and cultivate friendships. Girlfriends are a very important component to surviving midlife motherhood. Learn to say yes when someone asks if you need help, and return the favor whenever possible.

Confronting the Changes in Your Relationship

Despite all our resolve to not let the addition of a child change our relationship with our partner, it's inevitable that the relationship will change. Once that baby is here our partner is no longer just ours. Another role is added, that of Mommy or Daddy, and you will never think of your partner in quite the same way again. Now you have to share. (And, so do they!)

More than just our roles change after we have children. Both the quality and quantity of time we have with our partner also changes. Little eyes and ears are always around. You can't just take off for the weekend or have sex on the piano. New parents cry the blues, "Where's my life gone?" or "How can such a small person change everything so completely?" It's not that children change everything, as much as we change after the children arrive.

One new mom told me a story about how she and her husband, both professionals and well into their thirties and forties, tripped a little on their way to becoming parents for the first time. Like many new mothers at midlife she had read all kinds of books to prepare her for every aspect of motherhood. She approached this with the same diligence she approached her career. She wanted to be ready. She didn't want to be caught off-guard. Some of the books she read said, "Your first night at home with your new baby may be hectic and trying." Her pediatrician warned her about that, too. "I thought, *how tough can it be?*" she told me. "We feed the baby, diaper her, hold her when she's crying, and generally attend to her needs. What's so difficult about that? I want to do those things. I'm looking forward to it."

"At about ten that first night," she went on to say, "the baby started to cry. And the cries intensify. We pick her up and it does nothing to stop the crying. She's been fed. Her diaper's been changed. We can't imagine what's causing this great upset. Then we notice she's bleeding around the area where her umbilical cord was cut. Her stomach heaves up and down because she's crying so much and that makes the bleeding worse. Understand, in retrospect, this was not a great amount of blood. But, *any* blood on a tiny baby . . . on *your* baby . . . looks like a lot. My husband and I are calm at first. Quickly, though, we work ourselves into a state of semipanic, thinking this is a crisis. We're each asking the other, 'What should we do?' Neither has an answer. We're both on the verge of tears. Our nerves are frayed. It's late at night and we're at a complete loss when it comes to stopping the bleeding and quieting the baby. There's something about having to call the pediatrician on that first night home that makes you feel as though you don't have a clue about how to be a parent. He very gently and patiently calms us down. He says it's nothing to worry about, but to feel free to call back later if we need to. It's very comforting. Minutes after we hang up the phone, the bleeding stops and the baby falls asleep, worn out from all that crying."

If there's a lesson to this story, it's that no amount of experience in any other aspect of life can truly prepare you for what you'll encounter as a new parent. Midlife mothers, even though educated, well-read, and with years of experience in tension-filled jobs may still be overwhelmed by the uncertainty they feel as a first-time parent. You *think* you know what you'll be like as a parent. You *think* you know what your partner will be like. But, until you experience parenthood firsthand, you really don't know. You and your partner have been dealt a brand-new hand and you don't know how you'll play it until the baby is born.

READY OR NOT, HERE I COME . . .

There are some midlife parents who welcome the changes that come with adding a child to their lives. Natalie Hansen is one of them.

Natalie explained that she and her husband, Simon, had settled into a predictable life and they were ready for something new.

"We were *so* ready," explained Natalie. "Simon and I have been married for a hundred years. Our lives never changed, our careers were set. We *needed* a child. Not just wanted one. *Needed*. To make life worth living. And, when he arrived, we didn't care what we had to do to make him happy. So, we can't go away for a spontaneous holiday. For us, now the most exciting weekend we can have is a weekend with our son, Joey. He brings us such joy. We are counting on having more."

As you can guess, not all midlife parents have the same feelings of sentimentality experienced by Natalie and Simon. During our conversations, many expressed their delight, but others very honestly confessed to the difficulty they had in making the transition from couple to family. Here's one midlife mom who is still struggling.

"After three years of dating, my boyfriend and I did marry, and I was adamant about not wanting kids. We were doing quite well without kids. We enjoyed our freedom, traveled, saved money, and built very satisfying careers. I even acquired my law degree during this time.

"By the time we thought it was the right time, I was in a position at my job that required a great amount of time in court and travel. Then we found out that my husband had acquired an infertility problem over the years. IVF would now be the only way I could get pregnant.

"My first and last IVF cycle was a disaster. The drugs associated with the procedure almost killed me. I lost ten pounds in a week and landed in the hospital for a few days. With IVF out of the question, my husband and I decided to adopt. We finally found our darling little girl when I was thirty-eight, and started the procedure to adopt her. While doing so, I became pregnant! The pregnancy and delivery were great, but I now have two children that are *very* close in age.

"It has been very difficult to have children less than a year apart, but I love my children, that's not the problem. The problem is, I really resent my husband. Since we adopted our daughter, he has not been there emotionally. He was supposed to take a week off the week we got her. The morning after she arrived he went back to work. He never took a moment off to help me. After expressing just how hurt I was, he told me he would be there for me when our son was born. He was at the birth, but that was it. He went back to work the next day and I was left with a newborn, a toddler, and no help. And, it has never gotten any better. Since the children have arrived, we have no life together. His life has not changed since the babies. Mine, on the other hand, is nothing like it was. Every decision about the kids is left to me. I can be drop-dead exhausted and my husband will sit and watch me bathe one kid, diaper the other one, answer the phone, and cook a meal. I am very sad that my poor children have older parents. Why did I just not have them in my early thirties instead of late thirties. I am angry that I let him persuade me to wait. I don't know why. It would have been no different. I would have just been younger. I worry incessantly about my kids having old parents and that I won't be around for them."

Studies show that the most stressful times experienced by married couples are the first two years after a child is born. Statistics on new marriages report that one in eight couples divorce or separate before the new baby even reaches eighteen months of age. These stats can be discouraging to parents who first rejoice at the addition of a child, only to find the changes brought on by that addition are devastating to their relationship. Taking a proactive approach, anticipating problems and looking for solutions early on, may help prevent trouble as your marriage moves on to the next level.

Experts tell us that a difference in how parents discipline their children is another of the primary reasons couples divorce. Knowing this, it's a good idea to anticipate disagreements and come to a mutual decision about how you will discipline your child *before* you are faced with a disciplinary problem.

Another hat I wear that I have not previously mentioned is that I am certified mediator for stepfamily and custody issues. I see conflict over disciplinary tactics every day. When I have suggested an early discussion about discipline to parents of young children, some laugh. "Discipline?" they say. "My child is only a newborn. We won't have to worry about discipline for years." That's probably true, and that's why it is so important to discuss these things early on. Couples who have had a few years of raising a baby together are often surprised by the arguments that ensue when adding discipline to the equation. Head off problems before they happen to ensure that your relationship won't be added to the divorce statistics. Here are a few questions to help you anticipate what is ahead:

* **DISCUSS PARTICULAR SITUATIONS.** Get specific. For example: "If Johnny won't go to sleep, will we go to his room to soothe him in his own bed, or will we bring him into ours?" A difference in opinion on how to handle this one has caused many an argument in couples of any age.

* **WILL WE SPANK OUR CHILD?** If parents who spanked raised you and your partner was raised by parents who didn't, this can be a huge subject for discussion. Figure this one out before you are confronted with an issue.

* **WHAT CAN WE BOTH DO TO STAY CONSISTENT IN OUR DISCI-PLINARY TACTICS?** After you make a disciplinary decision together, stick to it. Keep communication open and discuss things with the other parent before you make policy changes.

There is more help on disciplining older children in Chapter 9, Roadside Assistance.

Good books on child discipline to consider:

How to Talk So Your Kids Will Listen and Listen So Your Kids Will Talk, by Adele Faber and Elaine Mazlish.

The Discipline Book: How to Have a Better-Behaved Child from Birth to Age Ten, by William Sears and Martha Sears.

Making Children Mind Without Losing Yours, by Kevin Leman.

1-2-3 Magic: Effective Discipline for Children 2–12, by Thomas W. Phelan, Ph.D.

Positive Discipline A-Z, Revised and Expanded 2nd Edition: From Toddlers to Teens, 1001 Solutions to Everyday Parenting Problems, by Jane Nelsen, et al.

When 'No' Gets You Nowhere: Teaching Your Toddler and Child Self-Control, by Mark L. Brenner.

SEX AND INTIMACY: A THING OF THE PAST?

Do you remember a time when you were in perfect sync with your partner? When you finished each other's sentences? When there were times you didn't have to speak to explain how you were feeling? Then a baby was added, and that mysterious rhythm of intimacy that previously came so naturally seemed to disappear. And our perceptions seem to change. For example, ask a couple what was most impacted by their having a child and both partners will mention the same two things, but not in the same order. The mother will most often answer, sleep and sex, while her partner will most often answer, sex and sleep. It's the paradox of parenting, and there is no easy solution.

This parenting paradox seems to be exaggerated for a new mother at midlife. For these women, having a child has only intensified their midlife exhaustion. Add those postpregnancy hormones gone haywire, coupled with approaching perimenopause, and it's understandable if sex isn't first and foremost on your list.

The following confessions are the uncensored comments of midlife mothers facing shifting hormones, more bodies in the house, and partners who may not understand all the changes they are going through. I'm sure, somewhere, you will see a glimmer of personal recollection. The first one is my favorite.

"I don't even call my husband by his first name anymore," says Melissa, sighing, a midlife mother of a toddler. "I refer to him as Daddy. Heck, he refers to himself as Daddy! I was listening to him talk to our son yesterday? 'Son,' he said. 'Daddy is not happy with you.' No one has first names anymore. We're Daddy and Mommy. It's difficult to get sexy with someone you call 'Daddy.' He makes a joke about it and calls out 'Who's your Daddy?' at the appropriate time. Doesn't turn me on. I go out of my way now to call him Jeff when we are naked."

For some reason sex and intimacy are always mentioned in the same breath, but ask a midlife mother and she will tell you the two don't necessarily go hand-in-hand.

"I am far more intimate with my child than I am with my husband," admitted Ann Marie, an attorney and first-time mother at midlife. Ann Marie's son is the culmination of six years of fertility treatments. She has not conceived again, even using the same treatments that resulted in the birth of her son. "My son and I can lie on the bed for hours cuddling and cooing, watching TV or reading a story. If I did that with my husband, in five minutes he would want to have sex and then I would spend the next fifteen minutes fighting him off. Then I'm mad and have no desire to do it, anyway. So I find ways to not be in the same room when we are alone. That's sad, isn't it? I didn't realize I was doing it until this conversation. I guess I do have some things to work through. My husband says I act like I am always angry with him, and he's probably right. I resent that I can't be close to him. As soon as I let my guard down, he's right there with a hard-on. I would like him to distinguish the difference between intimacy and sex, but he can't, so for me, I find that intimacy with my son."

And there lies the rub. Men think intimacy *is* sex. Women think intimacy is being emotionally close. I went so far as to look up the word *intimacy* in my thesaurus. It listed the words *familiarity*, *closeness*, *understanding*, *relationship*, and *confidence*. A woman must have written my thesaurus. The word *sex* was not listed.

When one woman brought up this subject with her husband, he asked, "How can you feel close if there's no sex?" The thing that many men don't understand is, if you offer *intimacy* to a woman, sex will mostly likely follow. And, conversation, especially listening, can be a very sexy form of foreplay, at least to a new mother craving adult attention.

THE BIG DIFFERENCE . . .

I have had two separate lives, really. I was married the first time when I was younger, but neither my ex-husband nor I tended to our relationship and it eventually became something neither of us wanted. We had a child, but we divorced before she was even one. I was a single mom and I waited for a long time to remarry and even longer to have another child. Now in my late forties, sex is not number one on my list, but intimacy? There's nothing like sitting close to my husband, holding his hand and listening to our little daughter sing us a song. She'll stand in front of the TV, tell us we *have* to listen, and then break into her personal rendition of whatever song is popular at the time. For a mom that didn't get to share the love for her child with a partner, this is bliss. And, sex? It's all part of it. On the weekends our daughter sometimes spends the night at a friend's house. We light candles, play music, and dance in our underwear the way we used to before she was born. It's the only time I'm positive she won't walk in on us, and I can relax and feel a little sexy.

TIPS TO KEEP YOUR RELATIONSHIP SEXY AFTER THE ARRIVAL OF A CHILD

We have all read enough pop psychology, gone to enough therapists, and compared notes with enough friends to know that, just like everything else in life, our sex life is what we make it. We also know it's up to *both* partners to keep the passion alive, but many couples, not only those at midlife, confide that because of exhaustion and preoccupation with either the new baby or older children, there is a tendency to forget about those little things that keep us coming back for more.

First Things First: If You Can, Get Away

Grace Ferrazi, a midlife mom at forty, confided it took a good year to return to pre-baby romance. Her solution was simple—to get away. "We try to go away for a few days, just long enough to get away from the kids and remind us that we are a couple. Even though sex is fleeting when we are home, we try to be spontaneous when we are away. The memories are enough. When we get home we secretly reminisce about our escapades and that seems both intimate and sexy to me."

Another midlife mom and her partner looking for "couple time" also go away for quick weekends, but passed on an excellent tip learned from months of worrying. "You have to learn to trust your caregivers with your children so that you can forget about them for a few minutes and be intimate once again with your partner. If you are constantly worried about the baby, it's not just the two of you. It's the three of you even if you are alone together, and that defeats the purpose of going away to be alone."

Making *It Sexy*

A lot of feeling sexy is mental, what you think about it, and the *planning* of an evening or overnight can certainly add to its allure. Here's a tip to help spice things up in a relationship that's slowed down by demanding infants or toddlers: When you plan a getaway with your partner, try splitting up the responsibilities between the two of you. You pack, while he makes the reservations. Don't tell each other what you've done until you arrive at your destination. Someone bring romantic music, while the other brings wine or candles. Surprise each other. *Plan* for just the two of you. And, when it's time to return home, there's nothing like that "Mommy!" when you walk through the door. Then you have the best of both worlds.

Lovers, Here at Home

Most of the suggestions about keeping the spice in a relationship began with the phrase, "Get away from the kids," except our life is *here* with kids, not *there*, without the children we wanted so badly. We need to find ways to remind ourselves that we are not only Mommy and Daddy, but also lovers as well—right here at home.

New to being a stay-at-home midlife mom, Linda Jorgenson was at first overwhelmed by her new routine. "I had a hard time continuing to work after my son was born, so my husband and I made some changes, down-sized our lives, and I became a stay-at-home mom. The one thing I do miss about my job was that I got dressed up every day. I remember walking in the door after a day at the office, feeling very professional and trim in my nicely tailored suit. I even liked the way my high heels clicked on our tile floor. I would set my briefcase down next to the door, then click, click, click over to my husband while he rested on the couch. Sometimes we made love right there. I just don't feel like that anymore in my ponytail and sweats with spit-up all over them. I had to do something to change my attitude so I convinced my husband that we should discuss our sexual fantasies. We made a ritual out of it. I put the baby down for the night. I had purchased some 3 × 5 cards and I gave my husband a stack of them and said, 'Write down everything you ever dreamed of doing.' I remember the look on his face. It was like, 'Really?' So we both spent quite a while writing our fantasies, and then we traded cards. First, he read mine. I had never seen my husband blush, but he did that night. Then I read his. Some of his were pretty gross, and we tossed them, but we have made a pact and we try to explore at least one fantasy a week. It's kept us going for about a year now. We may have to break out the old 3 × 5s again soon!"

If you read between the lines of the suggestions made by these midlife mothers, each was really talking about their individual effort to reconnect with the person they love after a baby entered the picture. They searched for ways outside of the conventional quickie to be romantic and bring intimacy back into their relationship. The *effort* is what made all the difference. That's what keeps the home fires burning and reminds us why we are together in the first place.

"I'll tell you the greatest aphrodisiac," my new friend Dana volunteered. "Now and then my husband and I end up at a club with friends. We get a baby-sitter and try to relax somewhere without the kids. We have been married for twenty-four years, but we didn't have children until we were well into our thirties and forties.

"My husband can't dance, which he hates me to say, but he's never been able to follow the beat. I love to dance, so half the time I end up dancing with my girlfriends. Well, one night the band played our song. You know, the one that reminds you both of why you are together? Well, as the music started all my girlfriends left the floor, but my husband came up behind me, wrapped his arms around my waist and started to slowly sway to the music, singing the words in my ear. He turned me around and we danced slowly while he was softly singing. He can still sweep me off my feet, even after twenty-four years."

Too often, we let daily stresses get in the way of our personal relationship with our partner, and then it's difficult to find the passion again. And, for many women, passion may not miraculously return in a few months after the hormones return to normal. It takes time. To once again find the passion in our lives we may have to go looking for it—if we do, our partner is sure to follow. Perhaps the best advice of all came from one of the midlife moms we have already heard from, Grace, when she told me, "I try to put the little one to bed early so we can be intimate, but if it doesn't work out, we have learned to take it in our stride. It's our life together that's important, and that's what I depend on—our life together."

SEVEN

The Balancing Act—
Juggling Work and Motherhood

"I will need to continue working—only because I make twice what my husband does. I really don't have any clue how I will organize it all. I sort of have a plan. I am fortunate because my company has a very good short-term disability plan that covers maternity leave. When my husband has a bad day at work, he tells me he's going to be a stay-at-home dad."

—DEIRDRE, A FORTY-YEAR-OLD LABOR AND EMPLOYMENT ATTORNEY

When it comes to motherhood versus career, we midlife mothers get a bad rap. The rumor is that since we have been working toward our career goals for so long, our priorities are misplaced and we will just fit our children in between our work shifts. On the contrary, the exact opposite is true. Women who have been dedicated to something for twenty years *know* how to devote themselves to a cause. We bring the very things that made us successful in our careers to motherhood; we take mothering very seriously and we are extremely devoted to our children.

Years ago it was next to impossible to find a company that would support you in your endeavors to build a family, especially if you were a woman approaching midlife. Thanks to legislation and progressive-minded management, most companies, large or small, now seek out women employees for their skills and intelligence. Family-friendly is the standard by which we measure companies, and pregnancy or child rearing while working full-time are no longer regarded as a deterrent to a woman's productivity or promotion. (At least it's not supposed to be.)

According to census bureau data, women now garner more than 50 percent of bachelor and master's degrees, 40 percent of doctorates, 38 percent of medical degrees, and 40 percent of dentistry degrees. Plus the percentage of women holding senior-level management positions within the corporate environment has more than doubled in the last ten years. In light of these statistics, it is understandable why human resource administrators predict that women will soon be the primary wage earners of the family.

But these statistics don't really talk to the personal dilemma of the new midlife mother. Granted, they support that we are capable of equal dedication. We can earn those degrees, and we can work our way up the corporate ladder, but once there, if we also want to have children, we, more than any other age group, truly have a decision to make.

A Surprising Change in Attitude

Most midlife mothers who work outside of the home before they have children have every intention of returning to work after the baby is born. Maternity leaves are well planned. Day care is in place. Nothing is left to chance. I have found, however, that this may be a temporary state of mind. When writing this book, I spoke to more than two hundred women, and the consensus was unananimous. Midlife mothers told me that after that new child entered their home, their priorities changed and the career to which they were devoted for years became merely a job. Many looked for ways to work from home or possibly telecommute two or three days a week. The working midlife mothers who forged ahead in their full-time careers did so because of finances. They had to work to make ends meet. Most midlife moms confided that their career had been extremely fulfilling in the past, but after their child, they began to ask if it was all worth it. A bold statement, and probably not politically correct, but my finding all the same.

Leah Franklin, a thirty-eight-year-old stay-at-home mom, lives in the Boston area, went to college, got her BA in communications, and then had a very lucrative career in sales. She summed up my findings perfectly.

"I have found that most of my stay-at-home friends are in their late thirties and early forties. None of us are actually pining for our careers, we seem to have more of a 'been there, done that' attitude." Exactly. Been there, done that. While younger women are striving for the top rung of the ladder, women who become mothers at midlife tend to decide the climb just isn't as important as it once was.

How Age Determines Our Decisions

Leah's observation is a far cry from the attitude of the working mother in her early thirties, and there's good reason. If a woman in her early thirties chooses to have children, then take an extended maternity leave until her children enter kindergarten, there is plenty of time for her to reenter the workforce. However, if a woman in her early forties chooses to have children and then take the same extended maternity leave, she is now approaching fifty, and her employment options change. Of course, there is legislation to protect people from age discrimination, but legislation rarely stops discrimination. It just makes management aware of the problem and brings the plight of the older working mom to the forefront.

Younger working mothers may have yet another advantage. They can plan the spacing of their children. If they choose to take only a short time off from their career to raise a family, they can space their children close together. If they choose to return to work for a few years in between kids, they can space them farther apart. It is not uncommon, however, for a woman approaching forty to take years to conceive. If we are lucky enough to have one child, it may take years to have another. Or, because we fear the onset of menopause, we are forced to have our children very close together. Both scenarios directly impede our ability to reenter the workplace in a timely fashion.

"Our plan was to have two children, a year apart," said Maureen, a forty-four-year-old paralegal, before she gave birth to her son, Tyler, three years ago. "I planned to return to work when the oldest was about three. I got pregnant right away with the first and we thought our plan was on course. We used birth control for a few months then started to try again. After a year with no luck, I contemplated returning to work, but my husband wanted to keep trying. Time just got away from us. I never did return to work, and we are now considering in vitro. If we go forward with that, my working days are definitely over."

After spending over twenty years in the work force, some fortunate midlife working mothers often assess their choices and choose to leave their careers to start a new life as a stay-at-home mom. Financially secure as they enter their forties, living on just one salary is not a struggle for these lucky few, and so they take the stay-at-home-mom route. "It was a new life for me," said Victoria, formally the vice president of marketing for a large construction company. "A complete adventure. Who knew I would be a full-time mommy at forty-four. Not me, I can tell you that."

Midlife Has Its Advantages

There are some unforeseen advantages to working toward a career before you have children. As in Danielle Hill's case, the experience she gained by working for twenty years at a software company and moving up the ranks to a national management position put her in the right place at the right time. At forty-two and respected in her field, Danielle was recruited by a corporate headhunter to join a well-established computer company as executive vice president. Her daughter, Megan, was just six months old.

"I thought I was going to have to work for the rest of my life," said Danielle. "My husband makes a great salary, but not enough to live in California. He was previously married, too, and he has three other children. Child support eats away at our income. But now that I got this promotion I will work for a few more years until I am fully vested in stock options, then I will leave to stay at home full time. I don't look at leaving the company as retiring. I look at it as changing positions. Definitely a lateral move. I work as hard as I can in my position. I plan to do the same as a stay-at-home mom. My daughter will be five. I will be forty-seven and my family will never again have financial worries."

And Its Disadvantages

Not all midlife mothers have Danielle's good fortune. The divorce rate has rapidly changed the face of the American family and forces women who were formerly at-home moms back into the workplace. Add to this the increase of single moms who are the sole supporters of their families, plus those of us who are married and must continue to work because two salaries are needed to survive, and you have quite a few midlife mothers who work outside of the home with no end in sight. These midlife mothers, just like all working mothers, agonize about how their time at work deprives them of time with their children.

"I never know if I'm doing the right thing. But, I don't have a choice. How do families do it on one salary?" asked one midlife mother. "I certainly make a good wage and so does my husband, but there is no way we could survive on just his income. And if we want more than one child? How could we ever afford it?"

Ironically, for some the decision to have a second child is the deciding factor to stay at home. Juggling one child and work is doable. Add a second child, and coordinating schedules can be a nightmare. "With one child at day care and one in kindergarten, I didn't know if I was coming or going," said another midlife mom. "And I just wasn't used to being that unorganized. Not to mention that the cost of day care for two children is more than I make in a year." Another midlife mom agreed. "We decided after we paid for day care for both our children I would bring home $160 a month. No choice there."

"I was robbed of my choice," Lorraine growled. "My ex-husband ran off with a coworker. He left me with our two sons. We tried to have children for a very long time. Then when we had them he decided he wasn't happy. Some sort of midlife crisis, and those kids he wanted so much are home with my mother or at day care and I'm working twelve-hour shifts to cover his ass."

I understand when midlife mothers feel that they are robbed of their choices. I'm not bitter as the previous midlife mom, but a divorce when my oldest biological daughter was less than a year old did change the direction of my life. Since I made more money than my ex-husband, I couldn't depend on him for large child-support payments or spousal support to supplement my income. I had to work to support my daughter.

Don't get me wrong. I did love my job, and I got a lot of personal satisfaction from being so good at it, but each time I dropped my daughter off at day care I agonized about not being home with her. I resented I had to work so hard. *How did I get myself in this mess?* I wondered. While I would eventually become distracted by my responsibilities at work, the first half of my day was always fraught with worry and anxiety.

During this rather turbulent time, I remember watching a television show called *Baby Boom*. It was a takeoff on a movie by the same name, starring Diane Keaton. The TV show starred Kate Jackson as a working mom in her late thirties, who, because of the death of her friend, was asked to raise a baby. The Kate Jackson character, like so many of us midlife working mothers, was conflicted and agonized about juggling her career while raising her child. She was tossing and turning in bed, and in a dream sequence, her front door bell rang. When she answered the door, there stood June Cleaver and Margaret Anderson!

"Hello dear," they said, and I cracked up. June Cleaver and Margaret Anderson, America's perfect moms, from *Leave It to Beaver* and *Father Knows Best* were standing at the front door. They were holding a pot of tea and a plate of cookies, and to this day, I applauded the brilliance of the writer who thought of this.

"What seems to be wrong, dear?" asked Mrs. Cleaver. Kate Jackson's character started to explain her conflicts with work and home and how she wished she could be the perfect mom, just like them. June Cleaver and Margaret Andersen looked at each other and then back at the Kate Jackson character.

"But my dear," said June Cleaver. "We aren't real." The background music crescendos to allow the next line to be savored. "I'm Barbara Billingsly, and this is Jane Wyatt. We are working moms just like you." Oh my, I felt better. This image we have all been trying to live up to? America's perfect moms couldn't even live up to it! I remember thinking I had died and gone to heaven.

Like many of the midlife mothers to whom I have spoken, I continued to work out of the home after my first daughter was born, but when my second daughter arrived ten years later I was more secure in my position at work, but also more secure as a person. I had nothing to prove to anyone. I had remarried, and my husband and I were in the financial position where we could live on one salary, if need be. When my youngest daughter was thirteen months old, I decided to write full time so I could stay home with the kids. It was a very difficult decision. Climbing up the corporate ladder was not as important as watching my children grow up, though, and I walked away from a very lucrative salary to be a stay-at-home mommy, with a master's degree that hangs on my home-office wall.

Respecting Our Choices

My career was so much a part of my identity that the first time I was asked what I did for a living after I no longer worked outside of the home, my mind went blank. The person asking me the question must have thought there was something wrong with me because I just started to stutter like an idiot. My mind kept flashing on what I used to do, but if I repeated what I used to say, I would be lying. All my life I had been programmed to work outside of the home at a *career*. It gave me a sense of purpose. Believe it or not, for a split second I saw Gloria Steinem and Germaine Greer's faces flash in my mind and I thought, *What the hell? All this just because I want to stay home now?* At midlife the birth of my daughter had completely changed my sense of purpose, and I was in the middle of a huge personal struggle.

A few years after I left my career, my husband and I had some financial problems and he was forced to close down a business that took him twenty years to build. It was very difficult for him and during a rather heated discussion about his "pride" he asked me, "Do you have any idea how difficult it is to have to stop doing something you have worked twenty years to build?" Of course he was expecting me to finally empathize with the pain of his decision. My only answer was, "Yes, honey, I do."

Jan Black-Owens used to be a local radio personality in San Francisco. She did the news and commentary on one of the news radio stations in the area and I used to listen to her every day while driving around the city. I was probably more aware of her whereabouts than most because we had similar names and my friends often teased that I was actually a closet radio personality. I probably heard that a couple times a week.

I knew that Jan married another radio personality in the area, Ronn Owens. Shortly after Ronn started to do the coveted morning show, I no longer heard from Jan. I figured they were trying one of those long-distance relationships, and Jan had moved on to bigger and better things in L.A.—trying to juggle home and work. As it turned out, Jan Black did make a move, but not to Los Angeles. She left her very lucrative career to stay at home with her children.

I didn't find that out until I began writing this book. I remembered Jan and tracked her down via her husband's Web site. My original idea was to interview her about juggling work and motherhood. Shame on me for not realizing that she, like so many midlife moms, struggled with the decision and then opted to stay home.

"I was thirty-nine," she told me, "when I took a three-month leave of absence to decide if I really wanted to leave broadcasting. I was very lucky that KCBS was willing to grant me such a leave and I was honest with them in saying I might not be back. That leave took some of the pressure off of me because I knew I could resume my career if being a stay-at-home mom didn't suit me. I'd turned forty by the time the three months were up and my decision was made. I have to say that being older and more experienced made the decision much easier for me. I'd accomplished what I needed to accomplish professionally and ego-wise—and probably if I'd been ten or fifteen years younger, it would have been an even tougher decision to make. Also, my husband was more settled and confident in his position so that lessened some of the tension we might otherwise have encountered."

Balancing Work and Child Rearing

At midlife, experience is our greatest strength. Couple that with our inherent creative spirit and you have women who have the ability to analyze a situation and come up with creative, if not innovative solutions.

When I met Jo Farb Hernandez, a midlife mom from Northern California, she was the director of the Monterey Museum of Art. She was actually the first woman to direct the museum, so when she became pregnant she wanted it to be a very orderly, planned transition. Her plan was to continue to work until a couple of weeks before the baby was born, work from home while on maternity leave, and then return to work as soon as possible.

Have you noticed how some people seem to glide through life? An obstacle is put before them and they seem to gracefully dance from the oncoming truck? Jo did exactly what she always said she would do. She had her child and brought the baby to work! She set up a crib in her office and nursed the baby for months, plus the museum docents, many of whom were grandmother and grandfather types, adopted the baby as their own! If Jo had a board meeting, the docents would fight over who would watch the baby! She continued to direct the museum for five more years.

"At that point I began freelancing, which I've done since," says Jo. "I'm continuing to do it, actually, although I did accept a new job at San Jose State University this past fall. Freelancing was great with a young child. I could be there to pick her up from school, and just work at night if I had a deadline. I did some major shows during that time, traveling all over the country."

Is it human nature to point out the negatives rather than the positives of a given situation? There are very few times that I can remember when I have come up with a plan for something I really wanted to do that relatives or friends said, "Yes! Go for it! What a great idea!" I usually heard, "Oh, don't go into that field, there aren't enough jobs," or "You want to do what? Don't be ridiculous, do you know the probability of being successful?" Rather than acknowledge her determination and drive, or ask how I could help, I told her she could never accomplish her dream of having a child and taking her to work with her. Of course, she knew better, and *made* it work. That's the benefit of being a woman at midlife in the workplace. We have the experience and creativity to conquer any obstacle.

Looking for Personal Solutions

Listen to the voices of three more women who have also resolved their personal work/motherhood dilemma with grace and a little creativity. Natalie has four children. Her youngest is two years old. Natalie approached her employer with a creative alternative. She shares her job—with her husband!

"I am truly blessed. My boss is great!" says Natalie. "I work from 7 A.M. to 10 A.M. and my husband is home with Mackensie. Then he goes in when I get home and works until 5:30. We both work at the same place. It is perfect for us. I still get my insurance paid for and vacation, sick time, 401K, and a bonus. I am hooked up from home and work whenever I feel the need. I get my coffee and donut every morning and get to visit with everyone. I would have had to quit if Mackensie were in day care or had a baby-sitter. We didn't know how our boss was going to react so we had already made that decision." But, job sharing seems to share the load and gives them both quality time with their daughter.

Josilyn is an elementary school teacher. She was married for fifteen years when her husband was tragically killed in a car accident. She had twin girls, age fourteen, and all three were trying to make a go of it without their beloved dad. By the time Josie was forty, the girls were off to college and to her surprise she met and married a man who had recently been hired in her school district. Her new husband was thirty-five, never married, and desperately wanted children. "I wasn't sure I could do it again, but then I said, 'What the heck? Life is made for living.' " How fortunate for Josilyn, she got pregnant right away.

Josilyn planned her pregnancy so that she could take her eight weeks of maternity leave at the end of the school year. "Then, with three months of summer, I had a full five months to stay home with the baby. I breast-fed, something I couldn't do with the girls because I had to return to work immediately. And, then when I started back to teaching I asked to be transferred to the afternoon kindergarten slot. This way the morning hours weren't so critical and I could work around the baby's schedule. The girls think I'm nuts to start over, but I have never been happier in my life. I simply cannot believe my good fortune."

Perhaps the most creative way to deal with work and raising a child was Beth Maloney's solution. She made up a job. "One of the really cool things about having lots of degrees is that you can pretty much write your own ticket anywhere you want," Beth explained. "I was very successful in my field, mostly because I was so visual as a woman in a man's work environment. I married when I was thirty-nine, and by forty-one my bio clock was ticking pretty loud. I wanted a baby, but with my hectic schedule, I flew all over the world doing research, there was no way I would attempt it. I knew if I wanted a family I would have to change my life—at least my job, so I could be home more.

"I sat down with a pencil and pad and started to ask myself questions. What would be the optimum position? What would the responsibilities be? Where would we have to live? And, slowly my perfect job took form. My final question was: Was this position feasible for any of the companies with which I was affiliated. There was one! So, I made an appointment for an informational interview with the president of the company. I explained my plan. I also explained why this position, if created, would be an asset to the company. I gave the president my salary requirements, and hoped to God he would call me back. Three days later, I got the okay! I had designed a fabulous position requiring a home office and I was free to start a family." Beth Maloney and her husband, Phil, had their first child when Beth was almost forty-four. They are currently trying for another.

Beth had some final words that she asked me to pass on. "If there is one thing I can pass on to younger women it is to get as much education as you can. Education gives you options, and then the world can be your oyster. I have a bachelor's degree and two master's degrees. I went straight through college with scholarships, and graduated with my second master's by the time I was twenty-five. After that, I never looked back."

The Child Care Dilemma

When I asked midlife working mothers what their biggest concern was about working out of the home, every one, without hesitation said, "Finding quality day care." Here again is where younger mothers have a distinct advantage over the midlife working mother. There's nothing like having a trusted parent watch your children when you can't. When my mother watched my oldest daughter, I never worried for a second. I didn't have that luxury by the time my youngest daughter was born. Both my parents had passed away.

After my second child was born I personally visited every child care facility in the area. I was like a fanatic. If I was going to leave my precious child with these people, they had better be okay, so I would show up unannounced, I would call just to see how they answered the phone and how long it would take for them to get another employee. I checked the bathroom facilities, the food preparation. I made sure all the toys worked, that there were no cracks in the windows, and after I made my final decision, I did it all again. Thankfully, I grew to trust my choice and became quite good friends with the owners. (When we became friends, they also stopped charging me an outrageous amount per minute for being late.) We began meeting socially, which made me even more comfortable with my choice because I grew to know the type of people they were, not just them in their roles as day care providers.

I have found the best approach to day care is to think of your child care provider as your partner. When parents and caregivers work together, they can turn child care centers into a great place to learn and share. Knowing that most mothers are anxious to some degree about leaving their child while working outside of the home, the ultimate goal is for everyone—provider, mother, and child—to be comfortable with the choice for child care. The final objective is for our children to have the best possible care in the most positive and stimulating setting we can find. Stay open and honest with your provider and address any concerns immediately. This will ensure a positive day care experience for everyone.

Tips for Finding Quality Child Care

Most moms are not aware that there is a central source of information for child care referral in nearly every community in America. These services are called child care resource and referral agencies, or *R & Rs*.

R & Rs are designed to help you find and evaluate day care facilities in your area. Most are nonprofit organizations that receive federal funds and have a close relationship to local child care licensing boards. This enables the agencies to stay aware of current licensing as well as who has recently lost a license.

There are now hundreds of R & Rs around the country. The best way to find yours is to simply contact Child Care Aware. Their phone number and Web site are listed in the resource guide in the back of this book. They will ask you a series of questions to help pinpoint the type of child care that best suits your needs.

If you work for a large corporation, there may be an onsite day care facility available to you. This is an excellent option if you are breast-feeding or have a short maternity leave. In-house corporate day care facilities are in great demand, and often have long waiting lists. If a company day care provider is your choice, it's best to contact them even before you are pregnant.

The following points are good ways to measure the quality of a child care home or center.

EVALUATE A CHILD CARE PROVIDER

Caregivers and Teachers

o   Do the caregivers/teachers seem to really like children?

o   Do the caregivers/teachers get down on each child's level to speak to the child?

o   Are children greeted when they arrive?

o   Are children's needs quickly met even when things get busy?

o   Are the caregivers/teachers trained in CPR, first aid, and early childhood education?

o   Are the caregivers/teachers involved in continuing education programs?

o   Does the program keep up with children's changing interests?

o   Will the caregivers/teachers always be ready to answer your questions?

o   Will the caregivers/teachers tell you what your child is doing every day?

o   Are parents' ideas welcomed? Are there ways for you to get involved?

o   Do the caregivers/teachers and children enjoy being together?

o   Is there enough staff to serve the children? (Ask local experts about the best staff/child ratios for different age groups.)

o   Are caregivers/teachers trained and experienced?

o   Have they participated in early childhood development classes?

Setting

o   Is the atmosphere bright and pleasant?

o   Is there a fenced-in outdoor play area with a variety of safe equipment? Can the caregivers/teachers see the entire playground at all times?

o   Are there different areas for resting, quiet play, and active play? Is there enough space for the children in all of these areas?

Activities

o   Is there a daily balance of playtime, story time, activity time, and nap-time?

o   Are the activities right for each age group?

o   Are there enough toys and learning materials for the number of children?

o   Are toys clean, safe, and within reach of the children?

In General

o   Do you agree with the discipline practices?

o   Do the children sound happy?

o   Are children comforted when needed?

o   Is the program licensed or regulated?

o   Are surprise visits by parents encouraged?

o   Will your child be happy there?

The information in this chart was supplied by the Evaluation of Your Child Care Provider checklist supplied by National Association of Child Care Resource and Referral Agencies (NACCRRA) and is © NACCRPA.

Staying Comfortable with the Decision

Most of us have struggled with the stay-at-home vs. work-at-office mom question at one point in our lives. When I worked out of the home, I constantly worried about the kids, and when I decided to stop working and stay home, I missed my job. It's always been a paradox, but I have found comfort in the fact that I'm not the only one who feels this way. Lots of other midlife moms have told me that they get a twinge of regret with either decision. All agreed, however, that the decision is one all moms have to confront, and how we stay comfortable with this decision is an individual search for our own identity and personal contribution.

"I know myself well enough to know that if I didn't continue to work after I adopted Tracy, I wouldn't be happy," explains one single midlife mom. "My career has been my life. All my personal relationships revolve around my job. If I quit cold-turkey to be a stay-at-home mom, I would have been a stranger in a strange land. I see no reason why I can't continue to work and also be a great mother." She continued with another thought. "And, I'd have no medical coverage. Reality can be sobering."

"Come January each year I start to analyze my life," says Chris Baldwin, a midlife mom of two boys. "I think about how much fun I had working, how smart I felt, and how I felt in control of my life. I liked contributing financially, too. But, staying at home with my boys has other rewards. I get my warm fuzzies from them now. I realize now more than any time in my life that I have to make choices. I *can* do everything, but maybe not all at once."

"Maybe not all at once . . ." For me, Chris's comment hit home, and I realized that perhaps the recipe to being that superwoman that we all want to be is not to try to juggle everything at once—home, partner, kids, and career—but that we have done it at all, and that we can pass that knowledge and self-confidence on to our children. Of course, some of us don't have the luxury of choice and we have to do that juggling act, but for those who second-guess themselves, who struggle with the question, "Have I made the right decision?" *allowing ourselves* to be comfortable with the decision we've made is the key. Find comfort in the fact that it is always a women's prerogative to change her mind . . .

EIGHT

Staying "Back in Shape"

"I try to eat healthy, but where I used to never gain weight when I was younger, since giving birth I find it harder to keep the weight off. I'm still relatively thin, though. And I usually exercise, too. I was kickboxing regularly until last spring when I had an injury, which still hasn't healed. So now, just as I'm approaching menopause, it's been kind of tough staying in shape. But, I'll be back."

—BARBARA MATHEWS, MIDLIFE MOTHER AT FORTY-FOUR

Mothers are always talking about how they have to *get back in* shape after the baby is born. They agonize, "I used to look like that, now I look like this." It's not that we don't know what's healthy, we do. Every doctor and study in the world has told us that a good diet and proper exercise not only extends your life, but also improves the quality of your life. Do we listen? Not really. We let daily life and its responsibilities get in the way.

There are three aspects to good health and staying in shape: diet, exercise, and a positive mental attitude. Each aspect is equally important and serves to support the other two. A good diet supplies the nutrients necessary for a healthy body. Exercise keeps your body toned and increases your endurance, and a positive mental attitude wards off depression, and, in some cases, even disease.

Not one aspect of this triad can be ignored. Good nutrition will

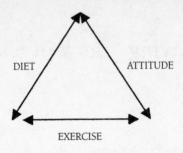

DIET ATTITUDE

EXERCISE

keep your mind sharp and make you feel better, but without exercise your muscles will not be toned and your endurance will be affected. Recent studies suggest that exercise alone can cure depression*—proof that exercise affects your mental attitude in a positive way. By the same token, a common symptom of depression is lack of energy. You just don't feel like moving around. Proof again that your mental attitude affects your desire to exercise. All three—diet, exercise, and attitude— work together for maximum health and well-being, and at no other time in our life is this more important than right now—at midlife. You have things to do!

Staying *Back in Shape*

The final straw to the one-of-these-days-I-have-to-start-exercising-again attitude was when I went in for a physical and was told my cholesterol was 235. I knew this wasn't healthy, but it was also unfair to my family. Then and there I decided to put an hour aside every day and go to the gym. I had no excuse. I live in a very small community and the gym is across the street! It was time—*again*. I was tired of thinking about getting back in shape. I wanted to *stay* back in shape once and for all.

*Young, R. J. (1979). "Effect of regular exercise on cognitive functioning and personality." *British Journal of Sports Medicine*, 13, 100–117; Gutin, B. (1966). "Effect on increase in physical fitness on mental ability following physical and mental stress." *Research Quarterly*, 37 (2), 211–220.

If you already eat properly and exercise, then this chapter will be a review for you. For the rest of us, it will hopefully serve as a guideline back to better health and well-being. I do not profess to be a fitness guru by any means. I am far from it, but I can say from my own experience, if I don't eat right and exercise, my mind feels dull and I have no energy, and with the hectic schedule of midlife mom, wife, writer, divorce and child custody mediator, and caregiver to an elderly parent, I need all the help I can get.

For me, the worst feeling I can have is when my mind feels dull. I hate it. I hate being in a conversation and searching for the words. Although I have been told this is attributed to perimenopause, I have found that my mental clarity greatly improves when I eat properly. So I have made a special effort to change my diet. Nothing profound. A little of this and a little of that from the five food groups that we learned about in school, plus I've added soy to my diet. Plus I've cut way back on refined sugar and caffeine.

As far as exercise, for this chapter I have asked "for a little help from my friends." Ginny Porter, midlife mom and someone you have already met in previous chapters, wrote a wonderful exercise manual called *The Pocket Trainer*. She and her partner, Jack Holleman, a certified professional fitness trainer, modified the exercises featured in *Midlife Motherhood*. The exercises are quick and easy and are designed specifically for the woman at midlife who is trying to get back in shape.

For the keeping a healthy attitude portion of this chapter, I went to the source, so to speak. I asked other midlife mothers what they do to center themselves and gain a sense of well-being. Put all three together—nutrition, exercise, and mental attitude—and we are on our way to being the best midlife mom we can be.

Start Out Right: A Good Diet

Because of the media and the pencil-thin models we see, we are all on a constant diet and perfectly healthy women think they have to lose five pounds. By the time we get to midlife, our metabolism slows down a little, and that five pounds has grown to ten, twenty, or more. If you have just had a baby, you probably wish it were only twenty pounds.

Personally, my biggest problem with food was simply the word *diet*. As soon as I heard it, I thought I was going to be deprived of some food I adored and I would never let myself get past that point. I didn't think about eating *healthy*, just eating.

"I was brought up to eat what I liked, and if I wanted to lose weight, I just skip meals to compensate," explained Marcella Gonzales, a midlife mom who wrote to me after she came across the Midlife Mother Web site. "I think about that philosophy now and wonder what was I thinking?" But Marcella's thoughts are the eating philosophy of so many of today's women. How many times have you heard a girlfriend say something like, "I pigged out last night so I've only had an apple all day today?" Teenagers are especially susceptible to this kind of thinking, and it's detrimental to your overall health and well-being. If you overeat one day, the next day you should eat sensibly, not avoid eating. To stay healthy your body needs nutrients every day.

I recently went to the doctor for my annual checkup. I love my doctor because she is about my age and has many of the same ailments about which I complain—the weight gain, hot flashes, but unlike me, her children are in college. Originally a nurse, she went back to medical school once her children were adolescents. As we sat and chatted after my physical, I asked her what are some things I could be doing to ensure I stay in good health. "Eat right," she said. "At your age a good diet is the single best thing you can do for yourself."

"Is that it?" I laughed. "Isn't there some medical advice you can give me? A pill I can take?" "That *is* my medical advice," she answered.

What Should We Eat?

A diet that contains a variety of foods will automatically supply the proper nutrients to your diet. As a rule, unprocessed foods are healthier than processed foods. It's best to eat fruits in their natural state to ensure you will get the most vitamins and minerals—a fresh peach, for instance, instead of canned peaches.

Now that experts know more about nutrition, their concept of what makes up a healthy diet has changed. Red meat is not as healthy as once thought. The protein supplied from red meat is important, but in smaller quantities than once advised. Red meat is also high in fat. We now know that a healthy diet consists mainly of complex carbohydrates, a moderate amount of protein, and very little fat. This little bit of knowledge is the root to many misconceptions about what are the right things to eat. Here are a few myths that need to be clarified.

Myth #1 Counting Fat Grams Is Better Than Counting Calories

Foods that are fat-free are usually packed with additional sugar, and although you are not eating fat, you are still taking in lots of calories. Too many calories per day translate into gaining weight, fat grams or no fat grams. For a diet to really work, you need to select low-fat, high-fiber foods that will fill you up—like fruits, vegetables, and whole-grain breads and cereals.

Myth #2 My Family Was Overweight So I Am Destined to Be Overweight

This is not necessarily true. The reason that being overweight runs in families may not only be because of inherited metabolism. It may also be from inherited eating habits. If you were taught to make poor choices when selecting foods to eat, you are probably overweight. Change your eating habits and you will most likely slim down and be far healthier than your relatives.

Myth #3 Fasting Is an Effective Way to Compensate for Overeating

Fasting can actually be dangerous and may not give you the results you desire. When you fast, the process forces the body to get its nutrients from muscle tissue and vital organs, not fat cells, and if you do not drink enough water during your fast, you could become dehydrated. The final negative against fasting? After the fast is over, the weight is quickly regained when you start drinking water again.

Myth #4 You Can "Spot Reduce"

If you have extra weight on your tummy, sit-ups will strengthen your stomach muscles but they will not reduce the fat in that specific area. The only way to lose fat in a specific area is to trim down overall.

Myth #5 Exercise Increases Your Appetite

People who exercise regularly tend to take in more calories to maintain their body weight. However, there is no evidence to suggest that overweight people automatically eat more when exercising on a regular basis. The key to weight loss is to burn off more calories than you consume.

Designing a Midlife Eating Plan

The U.S. Agricultural Department has designed the Food Guide Pyramid as a model of what is healthy for an adult to eat each day. If you look at it carefully you will see that suggestions have changed from years past; particularly the recommended amount of protein is now much lower.

If you analyze what the Food Pyramid suggests you eat, it seems like *a lot* of food. The first time I looked at it I thought I could never eat all that in one day—I'd be as big as a house! Then I realized that a serving size of fruits and vegetables is as small as ½ cup strawberries or ½ cup steamed carrots. A serving of protein is 3 to 4 ounces of chicken. Portion size makes all the difference.

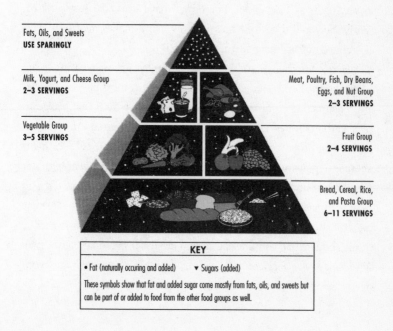

Fats, Oils, and Sweets
USE SPARINGLY

Milk, Yogurt, and Cheese Group
2–3 SERVINGS

Meat, Poultry, Fish, Dry Beans,
Eggs, and Nut Group
2–3 SERVINGS

Vegetable Group
3–5 SERVINGS

Fruit Group
2–4 SERVINGS

Bread, Cereal, Rice,
and Pasta Group
6–11 SERVINGS

KEY
• Fat (naturally occuring and added)   ▼ Sugars (added)
These symbols show that fat and added sugar come mostly from fats, oils, and sweets but can be part of or added to food from the other food groups as well.

Although the Food Guide Pyramid is a good model on which to base your diet, it does not specify whether the dietary recommendations are for premenopausal, perimenopausal, or menopausal women. A woman approaching midlife needs to eat differently to compensate for those fluctuating hormones and the slowing of her midlife metabolism. You simply can't eat like you did when you were twenty and maintain the same weight at forty. You need to design a new personal eating plan, and the best way to do that is to slow down and take note of how your body reacts to specific foods and different amounts of foods.

For example, I simply cannot eat refined sugar the way I did when I was younger. I love chocolate, but each time I eat it my ability to concentrate goes right out the window—within twenty minutes. I've been tested for diabetes. I am not diabetic, although, as I have mentioned, I was during my last pregnancy, so it is something I have to watch for as I get older. For now, I have learned I just can't eat candy the way I used to. Knowing how bad it makes me feel when I eat refined sugar, I have learned to pass it up.

Here's another example of designing your own eating plan. Although the Food Guide Pyramid suggests that most of your calories are consumed as complex carbohydrates, I feel better if I eat less complex carbohydrates and more protein than suggested. How much more? I eat protein at every meal. I have found the best ratio for me is about 40 percent protein and 35 percent complex carbohydrates (vegetables) and 25 percent fat. But I am forty-seven years old and perimenopausal. If you are ten years younger, your dietary needs may be closer to the Food Pyramid. That's why it is important to really think about what you are eating and design a personal eating plan that makes you feel good, adjusting the plan as you age and your needs change.

Healthy Eating Is the Key

The key to healthy eating is to eat regular meals so that your body is not *dependent* on snacks for fuel. Some experts believe the best way is to eat lots of small meals during the day. This could be true if the small meals are good for you. If you are just grabbing something of no nutritional value, it just adds to the problem. Studies have found that postmenopausal women seem to be less effective at burning fat after a large meal (over 1,000 calories) than women half that age. When the meals were smaller, we older women burn fat just as effectively as our younger sisters. With this in mind, as we approach midlife, lots of little *well-balanced* meals may be the most effective way to nourish our bodies.

The Truth About Eating Fat

Over the last decade, fat has developed a bad reputation. But the truth is that we need some fat in our diet to be healthy. The fats to steer clear of are the *saturated fats*. Saturated fats clog your arteries. Every day there is more and more proof that partially hydrogenated vegetable oils (which are artificially saturated fats) are detrimental to your health, both because of the artificial saturation and a side effect of hydrogenation called trans fatty acids.* Trans fats, as they are more commonly called, are found in just about everything from margarine to cakes and cookies. Because so many processed foods contain trans fats, eliminating them completely from your diet will be difficult but not impossible. Read labels. If you see *partially*

---

*Zock, P. L., and M. B. Katan. "Hydrogenation alternatives: effect of trans fatty acids and stearic acids vs. linoleic acid in humans." *Journal of Lipid Research*. 33:399, 1992.

hydrogenated anything, that's a trans fat, and a possible contributor to heart disease.

The Dietary Guidelines for Americans recommend no more than 30 percent of total calories come from fat. If you follow the recommendations of the Food Guide Pyramid, it's probably not necessary to count grams of fat or calories from fat. Just as a source of reference, however, if you're eating about 2,100 calories per day, 700 of those calories should be from fat (30 percent of 2,100 is 700). Since each gram of fat has 9 calories, that's about 78 grams of fat each day.

TIPS FOR CHOOSING LOWER-FAT FOODS

* Eating from the base of the Food Guide Pyramid is a healthy approach.

* Most whole grains, breads, pastas, and cereals are naturally low in fat.

* Fruits and vegetables *usually* have no fat. Avocados are one of the exceptions.

* Choose lean meats, beans, and low-fat dairy products.

* Cut down on processed foods containing partially hydrogenated oils.

* Watch your fast-food intake (fast food is notoriously high in trans fats).

* Learn to read labels to verify fat content.

* When cooking, broil, bake, grill, and roast instead of sauté or fry.

Should You Take Supplements?

Most experts will say, yes, it's smart to take supplements at midlife because there are certain vitamins and minerals we need as we age and we may not get enough of these from diet alone. The most important: calcium. Once menopause sets in, we are prone to osteoporosis, a thinning of the bones. If we do not have enough calcium in our diets, our bones will become brittle and break easily.

Most women get their calcium from milk or milk products; however, milk may not be tolerated as easily at midlife as it once was. It can cause bloating and constipation if you are not digesting it properly. I found that as I got older I developed a lactose intolerance, which made me cut milk products entirely out of my diet. Since I am not getting my calcium from milk, cheese, or yogurt, I take a calcium supplement. Most studies indicate that calcium citrate is better absorbed in the body than calcium carbonate, and doctors recommend between 1,000 and 1,200 mg of calcium a day for women approaching menopause.

If you don't take vitamins now, but wish to start, it's best to check with your doctor to see what vitamins and minerals you may need. Don't try to design your vitamin regimen yourself. When we do that we end up taking far more than is necessary, and some vitamins and minerals can be toxic when taken in large amounts. A simple, inexpensive multivitamin is usually enough. Your doctor can recommend additional vitamins and minerals if you need them. Now that I'm a little older, I tend to bruise much easier and small cuts do not heal as quickly. My doctor suggested I increase my intake of the antioxidant vitamins, namely C and E, and I have noticed a marked improvement since doing so.

If you eat properly you can get most everything you need from your diet. Fresh fruits and vegetables are your best source of antioxidant vitamins. Antioxidants fight cellular damage from free radicals, which has been found to be an underlying cause leading to conditions such as heart disease, macular degeneration, cataracts, many cancers, and aging in general.

Free radicals are unstable atoms or groups of atoms with an odd number of electrons. Since electrons normally come in pairs, an odd, unpaired electron in a free radical causes it to collide with other molecules in order to steal an electron from them. This changes the structure of these other molecules and causes them to also become free radicals. A chain reaction then begins in which the structure of millions of molecules are altered, possibly affect our DNA, protein molecules, enzymes, and cells. To prevent free radical damage the body has a defense system of *antioxidants*.

Antioxidants are molecules that can safely interact with free radicals and stop the chain reaction before essential molecules are damaged. Although there are several enzyme systems within the body that hunt for free radicals, the principal vitamin antioxidants are vitamin E, beta-carotene, and vitamin C.

It's always best to get the nutrients necessary to stay healthy from your diet; however, if you find it difficult to consume 3 to 5 servings of vegetables and 2 to 4 servings of fruits a day as suggested by the Food Pyramid, taking a daily supplement may be a good idea.

Estrogen Replacement at Midlife

There is so much controversy about the use of hormone replacement therapy (HRT) as we enter menopause that it is difficult to know what to do. This much we know for sure: As a woman ages, she produces less estrogen. Less estrogen brings on the common menopausal symptoms—hot flashes, vaginal dryness, and mood swings. While past research showed that women also needed estrogen to protect their hearts and guard against bone loss, additional studies suggest that estrogen replacement does not prevent these things and may be linked to an increased risk of breast cancer.* Proponents of HRT believe the benefits of short-term hormone replacement to control menopausal symptoms far outweigh the risks. The best suggestion is to discuss the pros and cons of HRT with your doctor.

If you decide that hormone replacement therapy is not for you, there are foods you can add to your diet that may help to ward off some of the unpleasant side effects of perimenopause (the time when you just start to show symptoms—your periods may slow down and you begin to experience hot flashes). Soybeans are extremely high in protein and calcium, and contain natural plant estrogens that closely resemble the estrogen made in the human body. A randomized, placebo-controlled crossover study of peri and postmenopausal women who were experiencing menopausal symptoms found that the women in the study who consumed a supplement of 20 grams of isolated soy protein with isoflavones per day reported that their menopausal symptoms were greatly reduced while sleep quality was improved.†

Soybeans can be eaten in a variety of ways. I buy frozen soybeans, boil them in lightly salted water, and munch on them like peanuts. I have also stopped using cow's milk and use flavored soy milk in my cooking and even on my cereal in the morning.

Miso is made of fermented soybean paste that is very salty to the

---

*According to a study by the National Institute of Health beginning in 1993 and involving 16,000 women, aged fifty to seventy-nine.
†Washburn, S. A., G. L. Burke, T. M. Morgan and M. Anthony. "Effect of Soy Protein Supplementation on Serum Lipoproteins, Blood Pressure, and Menopausal Symptoms in Perimenopausal Women." *Menopause* 1999; 7–13.

taste. It used in a variety of Japanese dishes and is most popular as miso soup, which served at almost all Japanese restaurants.

Tofu, or soybean curd, is another excellent source of soy protein. Eating tofu may take some getting used to; however, there is definitely a reason why we should make it a staple in our diet. In Europe 70 to 80 percent of menopausal women experience hot flashes, in Malaysia 57 percent, in China 18 percent, and in Singapore 14 percent.* Looking at these numbers it seems to say that the amount of hot flashes and other menopausal symptoms reported by women at menopause are directly proportionate to their intake of tofu and other soy-based products in the diet; the more soy, the fewer side effects.

Exercise: This Time I Am Going to Do It!

The first time I tried to go back to exercising was about a year after my daughter was born. I packed her up, complete with all the baby paraphernalia, and headed toward the gym. Even if it was just a short distance from my house, it seemed like it took hours to get there. Once there, I was soon interrupted in the middle of the workout by a teenage employee who didn't know how to stop a baby from crying.

Before I got pregnant, I was in excellent shape. I went to aerobics classes five times a week and I tried to continue throughout the pregnancy, but when I started to spot at eight weeks, my doctor said, "No more aerobic exercise," so I quit, cold turkey, and sat on my egg like a mother hen, afraid to move.

When I was in shape with a lower percentage of body fat than my lovely post-pregnancy body, I was used to seeing some definition in my arms and legs after two or three weeks of using light weights. Now I was far from in shape, and the routine I followed before I was pregnant was too difficult. Using a new routine I didn't see results fast

*Knight, D. O., and J. A. Eden. "Phytoestrogens—a short review." *Maturitas* 1995; 22:167–175.

enough. Disillusioned and frustrated, I stopped going to the gym, and I just got flabbier.

But, I'm not the only one. Most of the midlife mothers I've spoken to have experienced the same problem. First, they tell me, there's never enough time to exercise. Second, it takes too long to see positive results, they get frustrated, and stop exercising. When I was doing research for this chapter my favorite comment to "How do you stay in shape?" was made by a forty-five-year-old first-time mom. "Ha!" she replied. "Pear-shaped?" Could I relate!

Samantha, a first-time mother at forty-two, had this to say about exercise. "I exercised regularly before I had my daughter Celeste, but afterwards I kept telling myself that I would resume my exercise program, but I never did. In my mind I thought, I'll go back when she's three months old. When three months rolled around, I decided to make it six. After six I decided that the best time would be when I stopped nursing because then a baby-sitter could take over. Celeste is now a year old and I have yet to set foot in the gym. And I look so much like my mother I want to scream. But where's the time? It seems as if I get organized for the day and it's time to start dinner and my husband is on his way home. Each night I go to bed exhausted, thinking, 'Tomorrow I'm going to the gym.' "

A hair stylist I met recently while filming a segment for a talk show, spoke about her feelings about exercise after she had her first child at forty.

"Both my husband and I work, and right now there is so much work for me, I have to take advantage of it. This business is so up and down. Who knows? Next week everything will be shut down. I don't get paid if no one needs a hairstylist on the set. My family will be in big trouble! If I have a choice to exercise or cuddle in front of the TV while watching *Mary Poppins* for the fiftieth time with my child, my two-year-old wins hands down."

When my daughter turned six and was in school until after

two o'clock, I met Ginny Porter, and I was shamed into an exercise program.

"Weight-bearing exercise, Jann," Ginny told me. "Even a little will keep those perimenopausal bones strong. And stretching. You gotta stretch."

But I never know how much weight to use. Or reps? I told her not to make it too complicated. Ginny thought I was kidding. I wasn't. Make it too complicated, and I won't do it. "If you can't get to the gym," she teased, "start with cans of Campbell's soup."

I've heard of using soup cans as hand weights but really never took it seriously. I could see myself walking around the house pressing ten-ounce cans of soup. Yep, those bicep curls using ten ounces are murder. Ginny didn't see the humor in it. "You need to stay healthy if you are going to raise kids and go through menopause at the same time. An hour a day, three times a week, will keep you healthy. Or, start with twenty to thirty minutes every other day. It will give you some ammunition to combat the stress of having children at midlife. It's not like it was when you were twenty. You don't have to be model-thin, but you should be fit so you can keep up with your kids."

THE "I DON'T HAVE TIME, I'M A MOTHER" WORKOUT

The "I Don't Have Time I'm a Mother Workout" is very simple. It's a beginning strength-training program. If you use the program straight through, will you look like a bodybuilder in a month? No, but you will feel better. My friend Tina is a model. Tina's forty years old and the mother of three children, two of which are a set of twins, and she uses an exercise program very similar to this one designed for *Midlife Motherhood*. I would give it three months before you should expect to see some big changes. Bodybuilders use very heavy weights to build muscle mass. We are using light weights to reduce fat and improve our cardiovascular conditioning. The goal is fit, not movie star, even though movie star would be nice. But movie star takes lots of time, and that's the reason many midlife mothers are out of shape in the first place. No time. We can all find thirty minutes every other day.

To begin you will need a mat on which to do the exercises and two 3-pound weights. This exercise workout can be done any-where—at a gym, even in front of the TV. The goal was to make it easy.

This workout, in conjunction with a sensible diet, will help to keep your body healthy and at a comfortable weight. To round out the workout you may want to add some cardiovascular activity. Walk around the block quickly, keeping your heart rate up for a straight twenty minutes, three times a week, is a great start. Remember to consult your doctor first before you start any exercise program.

WORKOUT

EXERCISE: Squat

MUSCLE THIS EXERCISE WORKS: Upper leg and buttocks

SETS: 2

REPS: 10

COMMENTS: <u>Preparation:</u> Weights are not necessary to begin this exercise. Tina has built up her endurance and is pictured using two 3-pound weights. As you build your endurance, add light weights. Using light weight also helps to keep your balance as you squat.

Tina is pictured with her arms bent. If weights are used, this exercise can also be done with arms straight at your side. If you do not use weights, hold on to a chair or rail for balance.

<u>To do exercise:</u> Keep your back straight. Don't hunch over as you squat.

Heels flat on the ground as you lower body.

Hold for 1 second.

Rise to beginning position.

Repeat until set has been completed.

Rest for a few seconds.

Begin second set.

EXERCISE: Supported Lunge

MUSCLE THIS EXERCISE WORKS: Legs and hips

SETS: 2

REPS: 10

COMMENTS: <u>Preparation:</u> Use chair or rail for support.

<u>To do exercise:</u> Toes pointed straight ahead.

Keep back straight.

Lunge forward.

Hold for 3 seconds.

Regain balance.

Return to beginning position.

Repeat until set has been completed.

Rest for a few seconds.

Begin second set.

EXERCISE: Advanced Lunge

MUSCLE THIS EXERCISE WORKS: Hamstring and buttocks

SETS: 2

REPS: 10

COMMENTS: <u>Preparation:</u> In the advanced lunge you no longer use a chair for balance and you add weights for extra resistance. Tina is using two 3-pound weights.

<u>To do the exercise:</u> Toes pointed straight ahead.

Keep back straight.

Lunge forward.

Hold for 3 seconds.

Return to beginning position.

Repeat until set has been completed.

Rest for a few seconds.

Begin second set.

In this photograph Tina is resting the weights on her thighs as she does the exercise. If you find it more comfortable, this exercise can also be done with arms held straight at your side.

EXERCISE: Inner Thigh Lift

MUSCLE THIS EXERCISE WORKS: Inner thigh

SETS: 2

REPS: 10

COMMENTS: <u>Preparation:</u> Lie on your side, left leg slightly bent at the knee, right leg straight.

<u>To do exercise:</u> Lift left leg.

Hold for 1 second.

Use short up and down movements.

Repeat until set has been completed.

Rest for a few seconds.

Switch sides.

Do two sets on each side.

EXERCISE: Outer Thigh Lift

MUSCLE THIS EXERCISE WORKS: Outer thigh

SETS: 2

REPS: 10

COMMENTS: <u>Preparation:</u> Lie on your right side, right leg slightly bent at the knee, left leg straight. Place light weight against outside of upper left thigh.

<u>To do exercise:</u> Raise left leg.

Hold for 1 second.

Use short up and down movements.

Repeat until set has been completed.

Rest for a few seconds.

Switch sides.

Do two sets on each leg.

<u>Special Note:</u> Beginners do not have to use weights. As you build your endurance, add light weight. Tina is using one 3-pound weight for added resistance.

EXERCISE: Plie Squat

MUSCLE THIS EXERCISE WORKS: Inner thighs, hips, buttocks

SETS: 2

REPS: 10

COMMENTS: <u>Preparation:</u> Stand with your legs apart, slightly wider than your shoulders.

Toes turned out.

<u>To do exercise:</u> Lower body as far as you can comfortably.

Hold 1 second.

Rise to beginning position.

Repeat until set has been completed.

Rest for a few seconds.

Begin second set.

<u>Special Note:</u> Use light weight to start. Try one 3-pound weight and as you become accustomed to the exercise, increase weight to two 3-pound weights.

EXERCISE: Supported Gluteal Press

MUSCLE: Buttocks, back of thighs, lower back

SETS: 2

REPS: 15–20

COMMENTS: <u>Preparation:</u> Begin with elbows and knees on the floor. Back flat. Bend left knee at a 90-degree angle. Soles of feet at a 90-degree angle.

<u>To do exercise:</u> Lift left leg as you tighten your buttocks and push bottom of your foot toward the sky.

Hold for 1 second.

Return to proper position.

Repeat until set has been completed.

Rest for a few seconds.

Switch legs.

Do two sets on each leg.

EXERCISE: Torso Twist

MUSCLE THIS EXERCISE WORKS: Abdominals, waist, lower back

SETS: 2

REPS: 10

COMMENTS: <u>Preparation:</u> Sit in a chair that will not prevent you from twisting from side to side. Hold light weights in your hands, arms bent at a 90-degree angle, parallel to one another. Back straight.

<u>To do exercise:</u> Holding one weight in each hand, twist right.

Hold for 1 second.

Repeat until set has been completed.

Rest for a few seconds.

Switch sides.

Do two sets for each side.

EXERCISE: Abdominal Crunch

MUSCLE THIS EXERCISE WORKS: Abdominal muscles

SETS: 2

REPS: 15

COMMENTS: <u>Preparation:</u> Lie on your back with knees bent. Hands behind your head. Or, arms can be comfortably crossed over your chest.

<u>To do exercise:</u> Using slow and controlled motion, raise shoulders off the ground to a partial sitting position. Maintain muscle tension by not returning to resting position until set is completed.

Rest for a few seconds.

Begin second set.

EXERCISE: Push-ups

MUSCLE THIS EXERCISE WORKS: Chest and arms

SETS: 2

REPS: 10–15

COMMENTS: <u>Preparation:</u> Beginners start on your knees. As you become stronger you can progress to the conventional push-up position.

Start with arms extended and head up. Keep your back straight, body in line.

<u>To do exercise:</u> Lower your upper body. Do not go all the way to the floor.

Raise your upper body to beginning position. Do not lock elbows.

Repeat until set has been completed.

Rest a few seconds.

Begin second set.

EXERCISE: Bicep Curl

MUSCLE THIS EXERCISE WORK: Biceps

SETS: 2

REPS: 10

COMMENTS: <u>Preparation:</u> Begin by standing with legs apart, arms at your side. Hold a light weight in each hand. Tina is using 3-pound weights.

<u>To do exercise:</u> Lift left arm, bending it at the elbow.

Slow and easy movements.

Repeat until set has been completed.

Rest for a few seconds.

Switch arms. Begin second set.

Do two sets for each arm.

<u>Special Note:</u> Try not to raise your shoulders when performing this exercise.

Some Quick Notes About This Workout:

* Each exercise should take you about three minutes to do. Some more, some far less. This work will take you about thirty minutes if you do all the exercises.

* Start with the supported lunge and then move into the advanced lunge. You don't need to do both.

* Start with this beginning program for a month, then increase your reps to twenty when it feels comfortable.

* Weight can also be increased to five pounds after thirty days.

Attitude Is Everything

We have now talked about how important diet and exercise are to our overall sense of well-being, but there's more to making our life healthy than eating right and exercise. How we think, a positive attitude, rounds out our existence.

I remember a few years ago when I was out in the workforce making calls on various accounts. I woke up to one of those days when I just didn't look good—you know, the kind of day that if you fiddled with your hair for hours on end, it still wouldn't look right. The kind of day when the same makeup you put on day after day just doesn't sit on your face the same way it did the day before.

I was late, and it was my biggest account, and I had to get going, so rather than primp anymore knowing it would do no good, I took off for the day thinking, "Forget about the way you look. Change your attitude. Put something positive out there." I walked into my account smiling, probably smiling bigger than I normally did to compensate for knowing that I looked like a hag. The buyer took one look at me and said, "What's different? You look radiant." And, that taught me a big lesson. The smile is what made the difference. That's what people see first. *I* was far more concerned about my outward appearance than anyone I would have met that day.

A positive attitude is a cornerstone to physical health at midlife. Since some of us are not only coping with pregnancy, childbirth, and child rearing, but possibly face the emotional upheavals of menopause and elder care, too. Nutrition and exercise are important, but a positive outlook helps to center our soul and offer true peace of mind.

When I was a single mother (after my divorce) struggling to pay bills and worrying about how my child was when I was at work, I had migraine headaches, digestive problems, and TMJ (temporomandibular joint syndrome). Each time I had an ailment, I went to the doctor. One day, when my doctor slipped out of the room for a second I took a look at my own chart. Each physical affliction had a big *STRESS* written next to it, but my doctor never once asked what I was doing to handle my stress. He just prescribed medicine for the physical problem. I walked out of the office realizing that I had to get a handle on my life and my thought processes—what I was thinking was making me sick.

It's obvious that I had learned to internalize my stress, but it really didn't hit me until I had my youngest daughter. After her birth, I tried to continue to work outside of the home, plus be the mom at my house, plus help run a family business, and be a wife, not necessarily in that order. One day when I was stressed beyond belief I decided to call my sister. I will never forget what she said.

"Hi," I said. "I'm having a nervous breakdown."

"No, you aren't," she said. "You always say that."

"Yes, I am," I said again. I was trying to convince her that this time I was serious.

"Oh, man," she said. "I'm jealous. I've been trying to have one of those for years. How come you get to have one?"

I was confused. I was confessing my complete inability to cope and she wasn't getting it.

"Oh, to have a nervous breakdown," she said with a sigh. "I could go to a nice quiet hospital and sleep without anyone bothering me. No kids yelling, 'Mom, she hit me!' I could lie in bed and just relax. You could sneak in a bottle of wine and we could leisurely have a glass in the solarium . . ." We started to laugh and that snapped me out of it.

As you can tell from that story, my family has always used humor to cope, but I knew that due to the pressures of having a child at midlife and trying to integrate that child into an already well-established existence, I needed to find a way to center myself, and fast. I had changed my diet, I was exercising, but something was missing and I knew that laughing at one's plight simply wasn't enough. Laughter certainly helps, but I needed a mind-set to carry me through so that I could be strong when everyone needed me. At the time of that phone call, I was about as centered as a bowl of Jell-O.

Sooner or later, we all realize that we have to find our center in order to be what we really want to be—the best for our partners, our children, and ourselves. We all use different methods to cope. Some midlife mothers have told me that they read, some exercise, some pray, one woman said she "sings Motown really loud." I loved that one. I use self-hypnosis and meditation. I find at least twenty minutes a day to stop, breathe, meditate, pray, and mentally put before me what I want to achieve for the day, the week, the month. If I don't do this, with my hectic schedule, I feel completely out of control. And it helps me to get a handle on the chaos that my perimenopausal hormones seem to create without my consent.

We midlife mothers can be a philosophical bunch. If you have been reading along, you have already met some incredible women—inspirational women and mothers who have a special philosophy of life that helps to carry them through their days. Take Barbara Curtis, for example. Rather than become overwhelmed at the prospect of having a child with Down syndrome, she adopted three more. Or, the lovely philosophy of Susie Kevorkian and Janet Nunan—when talking about their path to having twins through surrogacy, Janet replied, "The babies are wonderful, but the journey was the real blessing."

Barbara, Susie, and Janet rose above the disappointments of everyday life. I was interested in what led them to their answers, so I asked them and other midlife mothers, and on the next pages you will hear from some of the most insightful, intelligent women I have ever had the pleasure to meet.

I began my quest by asking Barbara Curtis what she did to center herself. She told me, "Mine is pretty simple, really. I had years and years of doing my own thing and being selfish. I found it brought me no lasting satisfaction. I live now to serve others. I know that's weird in today's culture, but I know from experience that disciplining myself to put the needs of others before my own does bring great and lasting satisfaction—and lots more energy."

Darcie Johnston

"Staying centered after the birth of a child is impossible, no matter what age you are. I had my first child at twenty-three. Sister, I was prepared. I had read every book about childbirth and nursing and baby care and motherhood. But the one thing that was never mentioned in the books and that had never been mentioned by my mother or aunts or women friends with children and the one thing I was completely unprepared for was not being able to focus on anything for more than a few moments at a time. If you aren't actually doing something with the baby, which takes most of the time for at least the first year, you are at least thinking about the baby. Life is lived in five-minute intervals. For someone who is used to concentrating for many hours uninterrupted, for someone whose preferred style is that kind of single-mindedness of purpose, this is a shock—and torture!

"I remember feeling like I was starting to get my mind back when my son was about a year old. Part of that was because I had developed the ability to keep my mind on two things as once, like tuning in to two channels at the same time, a split screen. One half of the mind is always on the baby . . . Where is he? Is he safe? Is he happy? The other half is free to pursue whatever thoughts it used to pursue.

"When I had my daughter at forty, my life was a lot more complicated than it had been at twenty-three. There was a lot more competing for my attention this time. I'd been through it, so the inability to focus was no surprise. However, it was just as frustrating, and it was a source of real anxiety. Many other things required my attention: my sister's illness, finding day care, my son's high school graduation, my job, and so on. And then there were the projects that I dreamed of undertaking, if there could be any time left after obligations were met. I kept telling myself three things:

1. Relax. Do the best you can but try not to worry. The world will not fall apart.

2. This will get better. You know this from experience. Bide your time. You'll have it back someday.

3. Appreciate this baby, this gift, for what she is, because you have seen firsthand that they grow up in the blink of an eye.

Sally Mills and Gay Willbury

If you are a midlife mom, don't discount the friendships you can cultivate over the Internet. Both Sally and Gay are members of the e-group for midlife mothers that I stumbled across during my research. Both post messages regularly and are always the first ones to respond to a call for help. Sally lives in San Jose, California, with her husband and her son, Johnny. Gay is also married, but is on her second family and lives in New York. The Internet has allowed these two women from across the country to share their ideas, hopes, and dreams—and to become close friends.

"When you first asked me this question," Sally explained, "I wasn't sure how to answer, but after thinking about it, I believe Johnny's birth has actually centered me. He is the focus of my future. I stopped smoking because of him. I marvel in so much of what I experience with him. So, perhaps I do not have to *make* myself centered, it just comes naturally with help from Johnny's birth. Because of my age (forty-six) I don't tend to think about all the things I did with my first three children. They are all teens now, and I focus on the fact that my years are numbered and I *need* to concentrate on the overall picture of life, not worry about the small stuff. My life is more defined due to lack of time. I know I have lived half my life already, and for Johnny's sake, I need to work at making this last half of my life fulfilled and pertinent."

Gay was equally as insightful. "Having Amanda in a way was the slowing down—I think she is what keeps me on track all the time—there is nothing more relaxing than to sit with her curled up in my lap and cuddling. The only time I can say I really get to relax is riding the bus to work everyday—it is my chance to think without interruption or read. This lack of relaxation time is by my choice—Amanda will only be little for a short time. Before she was born I had many years of relaxing and doing things just for myself."

Danielle Dufayet

"Before I even start my day I close my eyes and sit in silence. From my heart, I give thanks for the following: my children, my family, my friends, my good health, my strong mind, my apartment, my job . . . all the way down to my bike and to the blankets that keep us warm. In closing, I ask for guidance in all that I think, say, and do. Then, I make up my mind to make the day as beautiful and joyful as I can. When things get me down, frustrated, or angry I remind myself that we are here only for a short while and that love is the only thing that truly matters. I make myself remember the 'big picture' and everything seems so insignificant compared to it."

Jeanne Cornelius

Jeanne Cornelius is the midlife mother of four daughters. She told me, "I'm am so glad I waited to have my last one. Being a little older made me see that 'this too shall pass,' and I don't respond to things so intensely. When I was younger everything was a catastrophe, and if there was a problem, I asked everyone under the sun for his or her opinion on what I should do. Now that I am older, although I still ask others when I have a problem, I go into myself to look for the answers."

Jeanne went on to say, "There's not just one thing that keeps me centered. I do certain things for different aspects of my life. For example, if things get too far out of whack, the first thing I do is hit the books. I read *Conversations with God* or other books like that to lift me out of whatever is bothering me. I also meditate to calm my racing thoughts.

"For physical fitness, I run every morning with one of my daughters. Of course, this helps me to stay in shape, but it's the time we have together that I regard as centering. During our runs we talk about our aspirations, discuss the meaning of life. She's sixteen and so wise. I love to hear her opinions and how she looks at life. It has taught me to be a better listener.

"My favorite thing to do is watch my daughters perform. I have gotten past being the nervous stage mother, so when they sing I can just listen and truly appreciate their gift. It is probably the most calming and centering thing I can do for myself, listening to my daughters sing. Their lovely voices were God's gift to them. And, they are His gift to me."

Phyllis Bowman

Phyllis, a mom again at forty-one, told me that finding peace of mind was a little easier when she had only one child. Now that she has two, she finds peace by simply asking for a little private time.

"The balance of chaos and peaceful moments is vital for me, and my answer to seeking balance in my life is to simply ask for some time alone. I send my older children and my spouse off for a few hours once in a while so I can enjoy the peace and quiet and just relax. After I have a little time to myself, the house is cleaner, and after some time alone with our little angel baby, I feel much more calm.

"After each child was born chaos was always more prevalent at my house, but I learned I had no one to blame but myself. I wasn't taking time to do what was enjoyable and peaceful. I found that simple things like going to bed early and allowing my spouse to handle the kids was an easy remedy. I think he prided himself on being able to get them both to bed. Of course, I'd make sure our newborn was fed, but then I'd relax.

"I have learned that focusing only on things as a problem gets me nowhere. At times, I'd just cry or let out my anger, but my husband stays calm and says, 'Okay, what can we do about this?' It has taught me to not dwell on the problem, but look for solutions."

Susie Kevorkian and Janet Nunan

"Every morning when I wake up, I count my blessings," says Susie. "I am grateful for the things I have, and spend no time thinking about the things I don't have. I'm a firm believer in the philosophy, Life is too short. Quit talking about it, and do it.

"My priorities are my family, children, friends, and God. How I juggle those priorities is the secret to my life's balance, and controlling the proper balance empowers me to make the right decisions. I feel that I am guided throughout my life to be unselfish and loving, and that understanding gives me strength."

Janet is a little more philosophical about how she keeps her life on an even keel. Remember, Janet is now the mother of twins. "In times of hopelessness there are several 'remedies' I prescribe to lift my spirits and keep me centered—my husband, my friends, my family, but most important, prayer. Each of these offers solace in some form. My husband by sharing my grief or happiness, as only we know it; my friends, namely Susie, in offering complete selflessness and a life full of joy and sharing; my family who supports me unconditionally; and prayer, a fountain at which I can stop for a refreshing drink of renewed hope."

NINE

Roadside Assistance

"I realize by having a child at midlife I have chosen the road less traveled. The future doesn't frighten me, but sometimes I wish there was help, a type of midlife mom roadside assistance— someone who would show up exactly when you need her and tell you how to handle the problem. That way the next time I hear, 'You're how old? And, your child is how old? But, what about the future?' I will have an answer ready for them."

—JANICE STEWART, MOTHER AT THIRTY-NINE TO JOSHUA

But What About the Future?

Ah . . . the future. Isn't that what everyone is curious about when they hear a woman at midlife is having a child? *"You're* having a child?" Or . . . *"You're* adopting a child? At how old? But, what about . . . the *future?"*

The implication is that we have made a mistake. However, very few midlife mothers to whom I have spoken feel that way. Most say that having a child at midlife was the smartest thing they could have ever done. It has made them look at their lives more closely, take getting in shape more seriously, and given them a second chance to do something really worthwhile. At a time when other women their same age may feel they are at a crossroad in their lives, midlife mothers feel they have a definite direction.

If I let down my midlife mom defenses for a second, my response might be, "Okay there may be a few extra things we need to consider," but then thinking it through further, I'm not sure what they are. If the age factor is a consideration because of longevity or illness, what parent does not worry, no matter what their age, that they might die when their children are young? According to the latest report from the Bureau of Vital Statistics, the average women now lives to within months of her eightieth birthday and the average man lives just about as long. Those statistics will only improve with age . . . and so will we.

With all this in mind, this chapter will offer assistance on subjects that we midlife mothers will face as we move down that road less taken. We will start with a discussion about choosing to have only one child, move to adding more children to your family, sibling rivalry, dealing with stepfamily issues, and juggling menopause, toddlers, and elder care. And, last but not least, we will revel in our choices and express our gratitude for our good fortune.

Older Parents, Only Children

Anne was chasing her four-year-old on the beach near where I live. It was early in the morning. She was one of the only people within earshot of my voice. When she caught up with him, she grabbed him around the waist, laughing. "Whoa, partner!" And that's when I called from across the beach, "So, how many more you gonna have?" She stopped dead in her tracks. "I'm grateful I had this one," she called back. "We're stopping here."

She could tell I wanted to talk some more, so she let her son run, and we met each other halfway. I introduced myself, and we plopped down in the sand to talk.

I found out that Anne was forty-seven, the same age as me. She used to be a dietitian for a hospital on the east coast, but moved to the west coast when her husband was offered a more lucrative job. That's when they decided to finally have kids. "My husband was starting a new job that paid quite a bit more than his last position. It was a new life, so adding a child seemed right. And I had been working as a dietitian for fifteen years. I felt as if I had already accomplished what I set out to do, so I had no trouble quitting in order to move. I had no trouble getting pregnant either, but after Robbie was born, we decided if we had two, I would have to go back to work because of the cost of day care. We could afford one for now, and then one simply became only. And that's fine. I don't want to start over again. We are fine with our choice."

"I hate it that my daughter is really an only child," another midlife mother told me. "Technically she has brothers, but they are more like uncles, fourteen and sixteen years older than she is. I came from a family of four kids, and I think having other kids around all the time helps you grow up knowing how to deal with all the slings and arrows. My husband *is* an only child, and he hated it. He was lonely and bored, and he was the object of intense focus from his parents.

"We have talked about having another child. But it has taken me four years to get any semblance of my body back from childbirth last time; I just don't want to go through that again. And then there is the exhaustion factor. We are already way too tired. I'm not sure I would survive another baby, especially if the baby was colicky like our daughter was. And finally there is that whole issue of getting my life back. Each time you have a baby you reset your trip odometer at zero. I am up to four now. I don't want to go back to zero."

Maybe that's what Anne meant when she said that she didn't

want to start over again. She, too, did not want her odometer again pushed back to zero. She was fine with the place in her life right now, and more kids are not in her plans for the future.

Waiting until almost forty or older to begin a family doesn't give us much time to have a litter of kids. There are, of course, the standard warnings against having only one child—because there are no siblings, there are no built-in lessons for sharing. We will overindulge them. Nevertheless, if a midlife mother is faced with making the choice of having only one child or no child, one child wins hands down, and we will deal with the inherent psychological problems, if there are any, when we are faced with them.

"Why Am I an Only?"

Susan Newman, Ph.D., social psychologist and author of *Parenting An Only Child: The Joys and Challenges of Raising Your One and Only* points out that single-child families outnumber families with two children, and have for more than two decades. "This well-kept secret," says Newman, "should help parents respond confidently to the question asked by many only children, 'When am I going to get a baby brother or sister?' More often the question sounds like a command, 'I want a baby brother or sister!' " Newman adds. "Parents' answers should be calm, thoughtful, and honest, and they should gear their response to a child's age. A four-year-old is unlikely to understand a biological clock explanation," says Dr. Newman, "however she will understand that you love your family just the way it is. It's important to reinforce your love and happiness, and most of all contentment. You might tell your child that she is all you need or want. If pressed the conversation can extend to the advantages your child receives because there is one child in the family." Dr. Newman also tells us that it is quite appropriate to say that families come in all different sizes and that every family is different—some have no mom, some have two moms, some have no dad, some have two children and some have five, but ours has one and we don't want it any other way.

"The good news is," Newman continues, "that generally somewhere around age eight, only children realize how good their lives are and the pleading for a sibling stops." And if parents need reassurance, the latest Census statistics indicate that one child is increasingly the preferred family size. "The bottom line," Dr. Newman explains, "is if the parents are happy, their child will be, too."

It appears the most common reasons only children ask their parents for additional siblings are boredom and longing for child interaction. In other words, they are lonely, especially if their parents are preoccupied with adult things and the child is left to his own resources.

"That's when I began to reevaluate my parenting skills," said Kathy Moraga, another midlife mom I met in my travels. "I came from of a family of five. I always had a sister and brother to play with. When we were bored my mother told us to go watch TV, so that's what I told my child. She got very lonely sitting there all by herself. I began looking for outlets to keep her busy, but also, so I could see what kind of activities she liked. I didn't want to be one of those mothers who forced their kid to play sports if they are not athletically inclined. I'm trying to offer a little of everything without overdoing it. I don't want her to burn out before she's five!"

Parenting an Only Child

Most older parents of only children understand their relationship with their child is unique. They either knowingly overindulge them—they've waited so long to have them, anything is fine—or they scrutinize their behavior so that the child can't breathe without being chastised. Parents of only children also tell me it takes some additional planning to stay one step ahead of the child. Because the only child's main interaction is with adults, they are often precocious and learn to speak early. Plus, when they speak, only children often sound like little adults, not children, and adults, often amused, provoke the behavior. Sometimes, it's not helpful.

I remember a time when I having coffee with a friend. My youngest daughter, who was then three years old, interrupted us. She may as well be an only child because of the huge age difference between siblings.

"Mommy," she said, "Steven is using *inappropriate* words in front of me."

(Steven is her older brother.)

"Really?" my friend asked, egging her on. "And what word is that?"

"Crap," she said matter-of-factly. "Mommy, how old do I have to be before I can say crap, too?"

Adding a New Baby to Your Family

The older your first child is when your second child is born, the more difficult it may be for the first to accept competition for your affections. This problem is not exclusive to midlife parents. It may be exaggerated, however, because parents at midlife tend to indulge their children, and a child of three may have every toy under the sun, plus Mommy and Daddy's undivided attention. Then, when another child enters the home, little Billy wants to know who's this intruder with *my* mother or father?

Sue Callen lives in a small town in Washington State. She tells me she loves her life, and as the words leave her lips, I can tell she is telling the truth. She starts to talk about her children and her eyes sparkle.

"I'm nursing the baby and my daughter comes up and smacks him right on the head. Shocked, I asked my daughter, 'What are you doing?'

" 'The baby's biting you, Mommy!' she cried. 'I want him to stop!' "

Sue starts to laugh. "Amanda is two, almost three, and we have had discussions about nursing. I nursed her until *she* was fifteen months old! She knows full well what the baby is doing. Her jealousy was a surprise to me. I expected sibling rivalry, but not such an obvious display. I found it amusing until I looked into Amanda's eyes and realized she was really hurting."

Go back in your mind when you were little and try to remember how you felt about your mommy. Not how you feel about her now if she is living, but when you were very small. There was no one better. Now think about how you would feel if the mommy that doted on you, that loved only you, now doted on another little child—someone that your parents are excited to have around, and they are telling you that you are related to this intruder! If you look at it like that, Amanda's behavior is understandable.

When bringing a new sibling into the home, anticipate what will upset the older child most, and then make changes before the new baby arrives. Try not to make changes that the older child will equate with the new baby's arrival. For example, if you say things like, "Now that the baby's here, it's time for the big boy to start preschool." The "big boy" might think he has to leave Mommy because a new baby has come to live at his house.

Addressing Sibling Rivalry

Children get very strange notions about why we do things, so strive to keep the lines of communication open even if your older child is only two or three. If you notice a rivalry brewing, try saying something that lets the older one know you understand how he feels. A good suggestion is, "Sometimes if a Mommy and Daddy have another baby to take care of, their other children think their Mommy and Daddy don't love them anymore. If you ever feel like that, please tell me so I can give you a big kiss. I want to make sure you always know that Mommy loves you."

Perhaps the most important thing you can do to ease sibling rivalry is to schedule time alone with the older child, away from the baby. This does not mean that Daddy (or your partner) takes the older child for ice cream and you stay home with the new one. If this happens often, the older may think that Mommy prefers to be with the baby more than him. When the baby naps is a great time to break out a book with the older child. Bake some cookies, play with clay, or color. Talk to each other! This will keep your individual relationships strong.

"Gabe was six and a half when William was born," explains Katie Murphy, who tells me her "major claim to fame" is that she has had three babies, all naturally conceived and perfectly healthy, in her forties. "We, of course, talked a lot about the baby and how wonderful it would be to be a big brother. Gabe really paid no attention. I don't know where I got the idea, but someone had suggested having the baby 'give' a present to the older sibling at first meeting. So, that's what we did. Gabe had been asking for a certain radio, real fancy with flashing lights and sirens. I found one at Toys Я Us, wrapped it up, took it with me to the hospital, and had William present it to him when my friend brought him to the hospital after the birth.

"Gabe's initial reaction to William was he wouldn't even look at the bassinet where the baby lay. (I'd also been told not to be holding the new baby when the sibling comes in.) He was glad to get the present and then as he was leaving I noticed him just peek over to look at the baby."

Katie listened to some great advice and headed off some bad feelings right from the beginning. Because of this, six-year-old Gabe did not have a long period of adjustment after a new baby arrived.

"Gabe was never hostile, just indifferent for a while. But it didn't take two weeks before he was happily holding his new brother and never showed a sign of jealousy since."

Special Considerations When Adding a Child to a Stepfamily

The subject of adding a new baby to an already established stepfamily was a favorite topic of the midlife mothers I interviewed because so many became mothers at midlife after having children in previous marriages. I had the longest pregnancy in history—for three years my family waited for our daughter to be born, and in those three years, my husband and I did our best to prepare our children (two from his previous marriage, one from mine) for our new little addition. We talked about the baby before it was born. We encouraged the children to express their feelings about the baby. My best friend let the kids help plan the baby shower. They attended the baby shower. We bought books and read to the children about adding a child. We thought we did everything right, but it became apparent that we didn't anticipate everything.

I wrote my first book about a year after my youngest daughter was finally born. My family had been weathering the ups and downs of family blending for about five years, and the older kids and I decided to collaborate on a book about divorce for children. We called it *My Parents Are Divorced, Too. A Book About Divorce for Kids, by Kids.* To write the book I interviewed my oldest children (remember, two bonus, one biological). I asked them what bothered them about their parents' divorce, and rather than saying "I don't know" or shrug their shoulders, because we were writing a book they were committed to honestly answering my questions.

As most parents know, children have a difficult time articulating how they feel. At times they may not even know that they are upset or depressed and can send adults mixed signals that we don't fully understand. During the writing of our book my kids talked about things that I had no idea they were feeling. One of the most eye-opening sessions was when my biological daughter, Anee, explained that she was very excited about the new baby, but also had a fear that I would love the new baby more than her. Her child-reasoning was that since I was married to the baby's daddy and obviously loved him very much, I would love the new baby more because I was no longer married to her daddy. She would no longer be special to me.

I felt terrible. How long had this little child harbored such feelings? She then explained that she now understood that I loved all my children, but she did worry for a long time. And, the hardest thing for me to hear was that she was alone with her worries. She was afraid to tell anyone. To this day I think of her face when she was talking to me and I wonder, "How could I have missed that?"

The fear expressed by my daughter is not exclusive to biological children. Years ago, while writing for *Working Mother Magazine* and now while editing a Web site for stepfamilies called Bonus Families (www.bonusfamilies.com) I often received questions from stepmothers surprised that their stepchildren, previously accepting and affectionate, were reacting negatively toward them after a new child was born. Sibling rivalry was expected, but never competition for the stepparent's affections.

This wasn't a surprise to me. I saw it happen in my own home. If you are privileged enough to have a good relationship with your stepchildren, adding a new child to the family can easily upset that relationship. The stepkids are jealous, and they are responding the same as biological children would in the same situation. They are afraid that the parent figure will care for the new biological baby more than them.

The best way to deal with this problem is to talk with them. Spend time with each child individually. Let them know you are there and that you appreciate them for who they are. Be consistent and don't lose your patience if the child acts out or becomes exceptionally needy. They are testing you to see if you really love them. A woman I've known for years confided that her parents had divorced when she was young. "And, when my mother remarried and had another child, I remember feeling almost abandoned. It was like, 'She's my mom, not yours.' Knowing this, I could only imagine how my own son felt when I added another child to our family. Until that day he was my world. Well, he and his stepdad, but even though my son was twelve and should have been able to understand things, sibling rivalry reared its ugly head. He barely looked at the baby when we brought her home."

From Only to Oldest

When a new baby is added to the family, someone that demands more time and energy than anyone else, your older child may perceive that he is no longer special in your eyes. Someone else has taken his place. To complicate matters, if he is quite a bit older and self-sufficient, he may be expected to grow up and help out . . . immediately! That's bitter candy, indeed, for a child who yesterday was doted upon, but today is asked to baby-sit. In essence, you are asking the child that feels rejected to be responsible for the very object that makes him feel that way. Resentment will only get worse.

Who Do You Love Best?

As soon as my youngest daughter could talk, one of the first questions she asked me was, "Who do you love best?" My first inclination was to give her the same answer my father gave me when I asked him who he loved the most, my sister or me? He told me he loved us both the same, and I remember that his answer did not make me feel better. I wanted to be special in my dad's eyes. Not necessarily loved more than my sister, but I wanted him to know I was exceptional. Every so often I would ask him the question again, hoping to get a different answer.

I think the "I love you both the same" answer actually promotes a rivalry between siblings. It puts siblings in a position to compete for their parents' affection. So, when my youngest daughter asked me, "Who do you love best?" I tried to give her an answer appropriate to her age that made her realize that I loved all my children, but I also saw her as an individual. "I love all my children," I told her. And then I continued by saying, "All of you are so different, I really can't compare you. *You* are so caring. Remember how you helped to take care of Gizmo (our puppy) when she got sick? And it makes Mommy feel good just to be around you."

When she was six, she asked me the question again. Now that she was older, I had the opportunity to talk about the individual qualities that make her special. "Each of you are special, but you are so different! *You*, my dear, with your freckly nose and sweetness are such a good friend to everyone. I just love your company. And you're so funny! You make me laugh!" So far, so good.

Did I answer the *exact* question I was asked? Not really; however, the answer she was given was the answer to the question she really wanted to ask. My daughter wanted to know if she was special to me, and that's what all our kids are asking when they ask, "Who do you like best?" They are asking, "Do you see *me*, Mommy? Do you see how special I am?" That's the question to answer.

A Common Dilemma: Extreme Age
Difference Between Siblings

Most child-rearing experts will agree that the ideal age difference between siblings is three years, but when divorce and remarriage are so prevalent in our society, it is not uncommon to find a ten-, fifteen-, or even twenty-year difference between the oldest and the youngest sibling.

At forty-six Diane Stephenson has had lots of experience integrating children into an already established family. She's been married for ten years to a man ten years younger. She came to this marriage with children of her own, and then added more. I asked her if she had any trouble integrating the older ones with the younger ones.

"Well, at our house the older two were fourteen and eight when the first little one was born, and then eighteen and eleven with the younger one. The older ones have always adored the younger two. There is the requisite amount of squabbling, but I sense very little jealousy among them. I find ways for all of them to spend time together, individually and all together, and it is priceless to see the alliances and relationships each has to the other. And the baby has just fit right in and taken her rightful place. We spoil her insidiously. But, hey! That's birth order for ya! She will be forty-five, and still be 'the baby.'"

This brings to mind another conversation I had with a woman named Lucy, a personal trainer from Des Moines, who has quite a different take on older siblings.

Lucy's mother was fifty when Lucy was born, and at thirty-seven Lucy feels no rush to have children. "There's plenty of time!" she says.

Lucy went on to explain that her mother was always an excellent role model, even now at the sprightly age of eighty-seven. "My mom is wonderful—controlling, but wonderful. She has been a stay-at-home mom her whole life. She tried to go to work once, but my father said there would only be one person working in this family—so, if you go to work, I'll quit. Probably the only time my father put his foot down! She's very intelligent, but only had the opportunity to attend high school. And, she still travels quite a bit. She makes being eighty-seven look like a breeze! And, she bakes the best apple pie in the world!" One of the things that struck me most when talking to Lucy about being a child of a midlife mother was how she felt about her distant relationship with her two older sisters. "One, is sixty-two, I think. The other is twenty years older than me. I'm not so close to either of them," Lucy said. "They've always been like more moms to me. Just what you want is three moms! They are very close to each other. I've never felt like I had much in common with them. They have kids—older or close to the same age as me. Weird, huh?"

I found myself privately wondering, "What kind of a relationship can siblings really have when they are twenty years apart?" Then I had to laugh because, you see, I have a brother that is considerably older than me and I know the answer firsthand.

As you may have figured out from various statements in this book, I, too, am the product of midlife parents. My father was married and had a son before he married my mother. My brother, Bob, is considerably older than I, twenty-five years to be exact.

Growing up with a brother twenty-five years older was a novelty for me. I think for him, too. I have memories of him picking me up after school and going out for coffee. We would go to this little coffee shop where he knew all the waitresses, and they would joke back and forth. He'd introduce me as his sister. I was seventeen, and the waitresses would lift one eyebrow. "Sure," they'd say.

Was I as "close" to him as my biological brother who is four years younger than me? Not growing up. Growing up, my older brother felt more like an uncle, but I knew he was my brother. He didn't live with us. I have no memories of childish pranks or arguments, but he was there all the same. He is family, and I love him.

My brother doesn't see our father as the pillar of strength that I remember. He knows a side of my father that I will never know, and he has memories that he occasionally shares with me. Sometimes I wish I knew the man that Bob describes because it would have helped me to understand my dad a little more. He was very strict, especially in regards to dating, but then he had a child at seventeen. Had I known the full spectrum of his past, I probably would have given him the same line my eldest daughter gives me—"That was you, I'm me." But, it's my forty-seven years of life experience that lets me understand why my dad didn't volunteer his life secrets. And now that he's gone, my brother Bob fills me in on what I didn't know. These days I appreciate my brother more than ever. He looks exactly like our father.

Influences of Older Siblings on Younger Children

I have only seen a positive influence by having an older sibling. There was no classic sibling rivalry, no childish bickering, but that's probably because the age difference was extreme. When my youngest daughter was born, her siblings were ages ten, nine, and seven, and the age difference presented no problem. As time went on, however, the age difference seemed to increase and sibling rivalry became obvious. When the children argued, rather than the younger becoming more sophisticated in her reasoning, the older ones actually became less mature. I found myself wondering where my sixteen-year-old had gone. They all acted the same age as the baby. And as the older siblings got older, my little one became more precocious than I liked.

The influences of teenagers made her far more aware of the opposite sex. At five she wanted to wear makeup like "Sissy." She wanted to wear crop tops like "Sissy." She wanted to watch the same TV shows the big kids watched. Needless to say, some of the common phrases used today by teenagers are completely inappropriate when used by a five-year-old. My biggest problem became how could I shelter my little one from the influences of her older siblings? I was at a loss.

Paula, a midlife mom I met at the gym, expressed the same concerns for her three-year-old son. We began our friendship on neighboring Stairmasters discussing the influences that our older teenagers had on their younger siblings. The first day I met her she told me the following story. Boy, could I relate.

"I was trying to get my three-year-old to pick up his room. I know he's young, but I wanted to at least start him picking up his clothes. He was doing everything he could to get out of it. He was lying on his bed, he was watching TV. He even wanted to take a bath, which is not like him. Finally, I said, 'If you don't get in that room and clean it up, you are grounded, Mister!'

"He glared at me, and flipped two fingers, like a backwards peace sign, about two inches from my face. I was fuming. 'That means peace!' I snapped.

" 'Yeah,' he snapped back. 'Piece of crap!' "

She was disgusted. "That's what comes from having a seventeen-year-old brother."

It is certainly frustrating when younger siblings learn "bad habits" directly from older teens. Especially if they are *your* older teens. It's one thing if the little one heard it from the big kid next door. Then you can go over there, confront the parents, mumble under your breath as you walk home, and fall asleep without any guilt that this was your fault. But when both the kids are yours, if you are anything like me, you are wondering exactly where you went wrong.

During a conversation, my friend, Dr. Susan Bartell, an author and a therapist who specializes in parenting teens, offered a few suggestions for midlife parents who have children with big age differences.

* **BE CAREFUL NOT TO BECOME ANGRY OR BLAME THE OLDER CHILD.** This will only cause him or her to resent the younger one for "causing trouble." In most cases the younger child is experimenting with this newly learned behavior to see how Mom or Dad will react to it and to see how it feels to be more grown up. The best way to handle problems in this area is to set appropriate but not punitive limits in the way you would with other frustrating behaviors. Watch that you don't overreact; instead, suggest some positive ways that he or she can emulate the older brother or sister. This is also an opportunity to invite a discussion about how the child feels about having a much older sibling.

* **BE CAREFUL THAT YOU DON'T FUSS OVER THE YOUNGER CHILD AND FORGET HOW THE OLDER CHILD FEELS.** It's not uncommon for the older child to resent the attention the younger one receives, causing him or her to be resentful and intolerant of the younger siblings. This is a legitimate gripe for many older children and, when necessary, parents would do well to provide a sympathetic ear, rather than dismissing these concerns.

* **TEACH OLDER CHILDREN AND TEENS ABOUT TOLERANCE, UNDERSTANDING, AND PATIENCE FOR A YOUNGER SIBLING.** Younger children admire and crave attention and respect from their older siblings and therefore feel confused and hurt if they are rejected. For example, if a teenager is furious that her five-year-old sister took her makeup, CD, or clothes, parents

can take the time to show her that she only did it because she wants to be just like her older sister. While this may not help completely, it will give the teenager an opportunity to be forgiving and to feel flattered that she is a role model.

* **PROTECT THE PRIVACY AND BELONGINGS OF OLDER CHILDREN** and teens by providing them with shelves and closets to store important belongings. Furthermore, younger siblings need to be taught that they can't touch things that don't belong to them or go in their brother or sister's room without permission. Older children that feel respected by their parents are much less likely to be intolerant of younger siblings. When mutual respect is cultivated, siblings can become friends even when they are separated by many years.

Older Siblings as Role Models

My husband and I explained to our oldest children that if we did have another child, they would be role models. Their younger sibling would look up to them and mimic their behavior, and because of this we expected them to take this into consideration when they made choices. I thought this was a brilliant strategy. Place the responsibility of being "good" on the shoulder of the child who was old enough to make good choices. However, I learned a huge lesson. When you place the *responsibility* of being a role model on the shoulders of older siblings, they may interpret that to mean that they are also allowed to discipline their younger sister or brother. Chances are a parent would not react the same way to problems that require discipline as does the older child, and it's important to help the older child see that being a good role model is different than being a disciplinarian. The younger child should look to the older for direction but not discipline. In response to her oldest sister's disciplinary tactics my youngest daughter confided, "Mommy, I know she's nineteen and I'm only nine, but she is my sister, not my mother." Excellent point. *Both* siblings have to remember that and it's up to us parents to draw clear boundaries.

Combining Past, Present, and Future Families: The Sandwich Generation

Traditionally when we talk about the Sandwich Generation, we are talking about women who wait to have children and then find themselves raising toddlers at the same time as taking care of aging parents. However, there's one more tier to this sandwich that is very rarely discussed. With all this marrying and remarrying and having offspring at different times in our lives, the birth order of our children is not as well defined as it was decades ago. Some midlife moms are having children at the same time as their children are having children. Therefore their children and grandchildren are the same age. How do midlife moms tie their past, present, and future families together? And, perhaps more important, how do we clearly define our roles as mother and grandmother when both children and grandchildren so closely interact?

The midlife mothers I talked to who were in this position were very conscious of the impact this phenomenon may have on their families. They understood that they were taking on more than the mere mother or grandmother role. Many are the primary caregivers for both generations, and they are far more active in the care, feeding, and discipline of their grandchildren than grandparents who went before them. And a few admitted that not all of them had the opportunity to rejoice in the fact that "after the day is done I can just give them back to their parents and they go home," because occasionally they all lived together.

Robin has been married twice before, and is now very happily married to her husband, Jerry. Her children span two generations. "My family is very close," says Robin. "My daughter and her son, Demetri, are at my house every day. My daughter is going to college full time, so I often care for Demetri during the day. When I had my first child we started to see a problem. My grandson was no longer the 'only' little one in the family. Now he had to share Grandma with someone that isn't going away, a baby, and this baby lived at Grandma's house all the time.

"If I remember correctly, Demetri wouldn't even look at Isaiah when we first brought him home. I think I even have a picture of the first look in the bassinette and he ran out of the room very upset! It took a long time for that to pass. I eventually gave Demetri a little trust and responsibility to be more independent, the same as if he was a big brother, and it really helped. Just today alone I have redirected jealousy a hundred times, the same as if Demetri and Isaiah were brothers. If Isaiah, who is fourteen months old, gets on a riding toy, then Demetri wants it. Isaiah has a sippy cup. Demetri had to have a big-boy version of the same cup because he wanted to be the same as Isaiah. I'm teaching sharing and respect for each other all the time, just as I would if they were siblings. Demetri is really smart, and like any older sibling he has figured out what works and what doesn't in order to get his own way. We know we have to be very careful."

Midlife mom Janet Northrup was just weeks away from her forty-fifth birthday when her daughter Cassandra was born. Her predicament is not uncommon in the world of midlife moms. "I am a grandma to four grandchildren. I have two older daughters from my first marriage and both were 'teen' moms. The oldest, my five-year-old granddaughter, was born before I even thought of having more of my own. I met my current husband shortly after she was born. We wanted a child together so we had our four-year-old son. My second daughter became pregnant with her son when I was three months pregnant. Her child was born a preemie, so our sons are six weeks apart. They each had one more child before I had Cassandra, who is two years old today.

"All our kids get along great, but it sure makes for a noisy house when we all get together! We get some comments, but mostly people thought it was pretty great that we are raising our kids together, until we had Cassandra. Then people, especially family, thought we were crazy to have one more at our age. Of course now that she's here they all love her. I have to admit, it's a little more difficult now that I am entering menopause, but I just take or leave the comments and let them roll off my shoulders now. I really could care less what others think. When I hear the comment 'I'm glad it's you and not me,' I just think, 'Me, too!' "

Okay, She Said It . . . Menopause

Juggling out-of-whack hormones and a little one is not easy, but doable. The mood swings are what really got me down, but they decreased as soon as I got my hormone levels back on track. If you know you are starting to show signs of menopause, the first thing to do is head to your gynecologist and have a blood test to check your hormone levels. Be cautious, however, if the diagnosis is menopause. I have found that most doctors prescribe estrogen or an estrogen combination to combat the hormone loss, and that may not be the answer for all women. There are studies showing risks as well as benefits from hormone replacement therapy. When the first signs of menopause appear, some of us do better with a more holistic approach, such as increasing the soy in our diet rather than taking medication. Work with your doctor to see what works for you. Personally I have tried three different estrogen replacement therapies and three different birth control pills. (Some gynecologists prescribe birth control pills to control hot flashes, etc.) I feel the best when I eat lots of tofu, drink soy milk, take vitamins, and get plenty of exercise.

Here are some comments from other midlife moms who have faced menopause while raising young children.

"I wasn't sad I was going through menopause. I was actually happy my periods were getting less frequent, but when I did have one, it was a doozy, and it knocked me down for a couple of days. I had a three-year-old that required my undivided attention and I didn't know how to split up my time."

And another midlife mom said, "At first the hot flashes didn't bother me. Really. But, then I noticed I got so bitchy that I found myself telling Danny, 'Mommy's sorry for being so crabby' about fifty times a day. Well, one time I snapped at him. He's five. And, I got this sort of look of desperation on my face. He put his arms around my neck and said, 'I know. Mommy's sorry she's so crabby.' It made me cry."

And, finally, a very frustrated midlife mom adds, "I can tell you from my own experience, hot flashes and toddlers do not mix. I often ask God why he allowed me to become pregnant naturally. You think he would not deplete our bodies at this time in our life, if we can still become pregnant. I now try and tell my younger friends not to wait past thirty-five to get pregnant."

So, what are we looking at? How does it really feel to go through menopause and what does that mean to your daily life? Polling other midlife mothers, not the medical community, it means the following:

* **SOME HAVE DECREASED PERIODS, SOME HAVE HEAVIER PERIODS.** Personally, mine are slowing down. My cycle has gone from twenty-eight days to about forty-two days, but I have friends who have periods every two weeks. Go figure.

* **HOT FLASHES.** You feel a slow flush, especially in your face, and it rises until you wonder if it's hot in there, or is it just

you. You may perspire, too, and your makeup melts off your face. It can be quite uncomfortable. My *younger* sister finds this amusing.

* **MOOD SWINGS.** As the estrogen swings, so do you. Remember how it used to be? Some days you are up, some days you are down? Now it's minutes . . .

* **LACK OF SEXUAL DESIRE.** Again, with the hormones. Could be a lower testosterone count, but your sex drive becomes non-existent. This one could be difficult to detect because you are so exhausted from chasing a child around, your sex drive may be nonexistent anyway. The only way you will know that a lack of testosterone is the culprit is to have a blood test. Then you can consider the appropriate medication and you are as good as new. Or not.

* **BLOATING OR WEIGHT GAIN.** If you are bloating, you're gaining weight. I went to college for that one.

A More Conventional Sandwich

As we age, our parents age as well, and as their health fails, our responsibilities grow. It's not uncommon for midlife mothers that may be caregivers for two generations to feel frustrated by their predicament. In the past it has been the grandparents who step in when tragedy strikes. If a baby-sitter was needed at a moment's notice, or Mom got sick and the house became chaotic without constant supervision, Grandma was there to fill in. But today's midlife mothers don't have that safety net. Quite the contrary, some of us must also worry, "Who will take care of my parents if something happens to me?"

What becomes clear as I spoke to mothers sandwiched between

two generations are the conflicting emotions they fight every day. On one hand they are grateful that their parents are still here; sick or not, at least they are still alive. On the other hand, mothers resent that their own personal time is now split into an even smaller fraction and that we are pulled in yet one more direction. They deal with a constant flow of opposite emotions—anger then forgiveness, frustration then relief. Watching one loved one blossom while the other withers, and feeling like we can do nothing but observe the process.

At forty-two, Janelle has had a difficult time adjusting to having a child at midlife. I learned that Janelle had a son in college, plus a new marriage, and most recently added her daughter to the fold. She continued to work outside of the home for the first few months, but received very little help from her husband. Her parents lived with her sister, who was feeling the stress of being their sole caregiver. She wanted Janelle's help, but Janelle was overwhelmed with her responsibilities right there at home.

"I sometimes feel resentful of my husband since he was the one who wanted children. This is my second marriage, his first. I have a twenty-three-year-old son in college. This is his first and only child. She has truly been a gift from God, but at the same time, I find myself sometimes resenting her.

"Recently, my mother went into the hospital, and now I need to help her out. My daughter is in day care and I feel guilty, as I did with my son, that I cannot spend more time with her. But when I do, I am exhausted! I have always been an athletic person, but lately I am feeling my age. I also feel that I am cheating her out of being the young energetic mother that I was for my son."

Melanie, a first-time mother at forty-one, has a similar story. She is the primary caregiver for both her eighteen-month-old son and her mother, who was diagnosed with Alzheimer's disease two years ago. "I feel so selfish that I get frustrated with my mother's illness," says Melanie. "Now that my mom can't take care of herself, and we can't afford assisted care, I take care of her. She doesn't get better, she doesn't get worse. All I do is change diapers—either hers or Cody's. I have no time for myself. I have no time to think. I feel so ungrateful to be talking like this. My mom took care of me her entire life. It's my turn to take care of her, and I am completely overwhelmed with the responsibility. Sometimes I secretly pray for her passing. Not that she will die exactly, but that God will take her. She's a shadow of what she once was, and I am in limbo. I'm not the mom I want to be for Cody or the loving daughter I want to be for my mother. It's just no good this way."

Like Melanie, many midlife mothers feel that they aren't doing a good job in either camp—mother-ing or daughter-ing. Even though they are doing everything they can to keep their heads above water, the responsibility of taking care of a toddler and an ailing parent is overwhelming. And, their desperation is only enhanced by the guilt they feel over secretly thinking things like "Sometimes I pray for her passing." Anyone who has been in a similar position understands they are not praying for a beloved parent's death, they are praying for their burden to be lifted—from both sets of shoulders.

There are ways to raise your spirits, however, but you can't put yourself on the back burner, as many caregivers tend to do. You have to take care of yourself, otherwise your frustration will increase. Here are some quick tips to help you juggle the care of both young children and aging parents. It's not rocket science, but as you read them, take them to heart. The first one is the most important.

Tips for Juggling Young Children and Aging Parents

* **TAKE CARE OF YOURSELF FIRST.** I know you read this everywhere, but it is by far the most important tip I can pass on. Exercise and eating right will give you the necessary energy to

cope with the extra stress of caring for young children and aging parents. The proper amount of sleep is essential. And, don't feel guilty about it.

* **IT DOESN'T HAVE TO ALL BE ON YOUR SHOULDERS.** Split up the daily responsibilities, delegate chores to siblings, older children, uncles, aunts, your spouse—and don't feel guilty about it.

* **BE ON THE LOOKOUT FOR SIGNS OF DEPRESSION.** It's not uncommon for a woman who feels overwhelmed by the responsibilities of taking care of a toddler and aging parents to become depressed, especially if she is not taking care of herself. If you begin to display the signs of depression—have trouble sleeping or want to sleep all the time, feelings of extreme anxiety or panic, feelings of inadequacy, don't be afraid to call your doctor or a therapist for help.

* **LOOK FOR WAYS TO GET A BREAK.** Swap day care. Carpool. Take a hot bath. You don't have to take everyone to the grocery store with you. I have been known to go to the grocery store in the evening so my husband can watch the little one and I can escape for a while. And I don't feel guilty about it.

* **DISCUSS STRATEGIES FOR LONG-TERM ELDER CARE WITH OTHER FAMILY MEMBERS BEFORE IT BECOMES AN ISSUE.** If you have siblings or other concerned relatives, now is the time to have a frank discussion about how you all deal with aging parents. And don't feel guilty about it.

* **GET LEGAL PAPERS IN ORDER.** Decide with your parents who should be named power of attorney and draw a will or living trust while they are still healthy and able to make decisions. And don't feel guilty about this either.

When a Parent Dies

My own mother died in an accident five years ago. I was doing a juggling act like all midlife moms, all the balls were safely up in the air, but when she suddenly passed, the balls hit the ground. Before her passing, I visited her every couple of weeks and I spoke to her every day on the phone. I depended on her understanding ear to walk me through my personal trials. Of course my husband was always very supportive, but there were times I knew he would think my worries were trivial. My mother never did.

As time went on I noticed that my mother's passing not only affected my own emotional health but also my youngest daughter's. (Mothers are the barometers of the family.) Although my husband and older children were clearly affected, they could intellectually understand what was going on. My youngest was three and my grief frightened her. Soon after my mother's passing, my sister-in-law, my daughter's aunt, also died after a long illness. There was no reprieve in between tragedies, and I needed to help my little one cope. This seemed like an astronomical project at the time because I wasn't sure how I was going to cope. Intellectually we know our parents will pass, but emotionally we are never ready for it.

Talking to Our Children About Death

As older parents it is likely that our young children will be exposed to death and dying far sooner than children with younger parents, and knowing this it is important to pass on the message that age and death are not necessarily synonymous. Situations will invariably occur that will allow us to introduce children to death before they need to face it in their lives. They may see a dead bird in the park or a pet may die. When winter comes, the annuals you planted together in spring will die and you can discuss the passing of time and the natural order of things. We can introduce death in literature, occasionally choosing a library book that broaches the topic. Your response to these teachable moments will reinforce that death is a natural part of life—it happens.

I remember a conversation I had with my youngest daughter, Harleigh, when she was five. By this time her fears associated with death had diminished, but the topic often popped up in conversation. We were on my bed watching TV together when she picked herself up on one elbow, and moved in close for a better look.

"What are you doing?" I asked without looking away from the TV. She started to smooth the skin on my neck, pulling it tight, then letting it go.

"Mommy, are you old?" she asked.

"I don't know, honey, do you think I'm old?"

Her eyes filled with tears. "You're neck is very wrinkly. Old people have wrinkly necks."

"Tell me about what you think old is, honey," I asked her.

"I think old means you are going to die." That was the heart of it. My daughter had her first sense of human life ending, and she was afraid her mommy was going to leave her. I hugged her close.

"So you are afraid I am going to die?"

She wiped a tear from her face. "No, you are brave." I'm not sure what brave had to do with it, but that's what she said.

"Honey, I'm going to be around for a very long time." I was preparing for the big talk, mentally trying to formulate my words so that a five-year-old could understand them. Harleigh dismissed me before I was fully into the concept.

"Yeah, well, Katie's mom is way older than you, anyway." (Her friend's mom was forty-four when she was born.)

"That is true. Have you ever talked to Katie about this?"

"No," Harleigh answered. "Her mom's neck isn't as wrinkly as yours."

My friend Marge Pellegrino, a children's author, took the death of her much-loved brother and turned it into a moving children's book entitled *I Don't Have an Uncle Phil Anymore*. Marge is the one I turned to when I needed some ideas on how to approach this subject with my own children. This is what she suggested.

"If we take advantage of the comings and goings of things in life around us—day moving toward night, the changing of the seasons, the moon going through its phases, we can be sure then that when children are faced with death, the concept won't be completely foreign. When a death does occur, how we talk about it, how we behave and address their questions will determine how they will approach death the rest of their lives. Here are a few of my suggestions:

* **TAKE ADVANTAGE OF FAMILY RITUALS.** After my brother's death my nieces at seven and nine were sent to school during the wake and funeral of their father. They were denied the community's outpouring of grief and support. They were shielded from the tears. Being shut out of the ritual made their grief harder and longer.

* **AVOID EUPHEMISMS.** Uncle Phil didn't buy the farm or pass away. He isn't asleep or on a trip. We did not lose him. He died. If you offer information in an open honest way, you'll give your child confidence in you. You'll naturally invite children to ask you the questions they most need answered. They'll trust you in this, which will spill over into other areas of your relationship.

* **BE WILLING TO SHARE YOUR TEARS.** While we don't want to overwhelm children with excess emotions, we don't want to

hide our grief either. Kids know. Masking or pulling back will frighten them. We need to show and tell him or her that it's natural to miss someone we love. Assure them that the sadness will pass. Balance that sadness with remembering happy times. Engage them in activities like drawing pictures, writing down stories in a memory book, and looking at photos and videos. Find or create a ritual that helps your family cope and grieve positively.

* **BE OPEN TO THE INNOCENCE OF YOUR CHILD'S RESPONSE.** Three months after my brother's death, my four-year-old son offered me an 'Aha moment' that helped me to move along in my grief. I journaled about my son throwing a ball up into the sky, to play catch with my brother one last time. The story jumped from the pages and became first a parenting article, and later a children's book. The process helped me let go. It also offered my nieces an opportunity to share in the rituals surrounding their father's death.

* **SEEK PROFESSIONAL HELP, IF NEEDED.** When we had three deaths in our family in a very short period of time, my son at ten became fearful of leaving me. He said 'I love you' fifty times a day. The funeral home counselor gave my son concrete strategies that helped him deal with his separation anxiety and move on. If you feel that you or your child need more direction, check with your place of worship, a school or community counselor, or organizations that help children deal with grief."

On Being a Motherless Mom

Even though mother/daughter relationships are often tumultuous, we cannot disregard the impact our mothers have on us as we grow older. Either we find ourselves acting exactly like them, or going out of our way to be nothing like them. Ultimately, our mothers are the gauge by which we measure our lives.

When I was younger I found being told I looked like my mother to be an insult. Never very hip as moms go, she looked rather dowdy, always wearing that outfit for "just around the house." How could they say I looked like her? I never saw it. But a year after she died and I was forty-two, I saw an image out of the corner of my eye as I walked by the full-length mirror in my bedroom. For a split second I thought, "Oh, Mom's here." I was seeing my own reflection.

It is said that when a young girl loses her mother, that girl actually loses a piece of who she will become. Women who put off having children are not young girls; their personality and outlook on life are already formed, but not their personal knowledge of mothering. No matter how old you are it's all new ground if you've never done it before, therefore, when in need it's a natural inclination to turn to your mother for advice. If she has passed, your primary role model is no longer visible, so you must look elsewhere for that calming reassurance. "You're doing just fine, honey. Your child will not hate you if you put him on time-out. You don't hate me, do you? And you were put on time-out many times." Where do you turn?

Women are great networkers. We are the first to search out a self-help group, head to a counselor, or even to call a friend when in need. Anna, a first-time mom at forty, lost her own mother but has become very close to her mother-in-law. "I don't think I would have entered this relationship with such open arms if my mother was still living," Anna explained. "I believe I would have felt that I was betraying my own mother by being this close to my husband's mother. But, my mother has been gone for three years, and my mother-in-law's presence actually lessens the emptiness I feel by my mother's death. Now my mother-in-law is the one I call upon for helpful advice."

I have a very good friend whose mother passed away only a

month before mine. We often find ourselves on the phone discussing things we would have normally asked our mothers if they were here. It's a secret club. No one knows we depend so highly on each other's advice and counsel. Our daughters, who now look to us for advice, believe we are wise and doing it all by ourselves. We are, I suppose, with a pat on the back from a friend, and heavenly counsel from one who was wiser.

In a way, the loss of my mother has added purpose and strength to my life. When looking for answers, I now must reach outside of what was comfortable and acknowledge my own good sense and life's lessons. This did not come easy. I went begrudgingly into my role as motherless mom. It seemed it came with no warning. I do fairly well, stumbling only occasionally, but there are problems that could use my mother's fine-tuning. That's when I put into practice what I was taught and what I hope to pass on to my own daughters. I accept, albeit reluctantly, that the baton has been passed to me.

Planning for the Inevitable

I think we will all agree that part of being a good parent means that we anticipate future problems and supply answers for our children. Understanding this, a discussion on wills and living trusts is worthwhile. It certainly made my life easier when my mother passed. Because she had a living trust, there were no probate considerations, and although her passing was difficult to handle emotionally, the legal aspect, the distribution of money and property, was stress-free.

When I asked other midlife mothers if they had prepared for the possibility that they might pass away earlier than expected, most did not like talking about leaving their babies, but admitted they had a plan. "As far as raising my babies," one midlife mother volunteered. "We have asked my husband's brother and sister-in-law to raise the children. Most recently my oldest daughter has said that she would like to do it, so I am very reassured that should something happen to both of us, our sons would be very well cared for."

"My eldest son has agreed to raise my youngest son," says Judy, a midlife mother who actually explained her plans before I even asked. She had her first child when she was twenty-five, her second son at forty-five. "I get asked this question all the time. I think it's strange that people anticipate the worse. Having this child was such a god-send. It has given my husband and I a whole new lease on life."

A *new* lease on life. Optimum word—*new*—the opposite of old. Attitude is everything.

Looking Toward the Future

When I think about the future and what I want for my children, I want them to have a happy life. I want them to feel loved. I want them to do great things, experience great things, and love things both great and small. I know that they will notice that I am older, but along with that observation I pray that they will see me as their inspiration, not someone who has grown complacent with age.

"I believe the greatest service we can do for our children is to teach them to be sincerely independent and think for themselves," said a very wise midlife mother. "I was forty years old when my mother passed on, and that's when I really had to grow up. I want my children to be more prepared than I was."

We all know our first responsibility as parents is to prepare our children to no longer need our direction, but it's equally important that we as their parents emotionally prepare for their leaving. For many of us, having children at midlife puts off the dreaded empty-nest syndrome. The bedrooms in our homes will not hold vacant signs until we are almost sixty years old and hopefully more emotionally prepared for our children's final ascent into adulthood. But we will have to face it; delayed or not, our children will leave. They will leave because that is the natural order of things. Independence is a double-sided coin. The supreme objective is that no matter what side lands up, we should both be winners . . .

> There are in the end three things that last: Faith, Hope, and Love, and the greatest of these is love.
>
> ST. PAUL

Epilogue

I believe that having the advantage of more life experiences and being more settled with who I am gives me a distinct advantage over younger parents. I think I pick my battles with child rearing rather than view every incident as critical and worth confronting. The wisdom and battle scars I have acquired over the years are available for reference and help me to adjust my perspective when addressing what seems to be an impossible situation. This was never more apparent to me than just last week when I found a treasured picture of my youngest daughter at three years old. It was taken during a family trip to a theme park/restaurant called Medieval Times. She's standing next to the queen proudly wearing the paper crown issued by the park. She is also wearing skintight stretchy plaid pants, a ruffled T-shirt, and her turquoise blue water socks that she called her fishy sandals. Her toenails are painted bright pink. Ten years ago, when I raised my first batch of kids, I would have never allowed them to go out of the house looking like that. We would have fought if the socks weren't color coordinated with the rest of the outfit. If my daughter wanted to wear her favorite boots with her favorite dress, I would have forbid it if they didn't match. I thought I was teaching them something about the proper way to dress. No plaid with stripes. No white after Labor Day.

As an older parent I don't stress. Of course I make sure she's clean and pressed, but if she wants to wear her fishy sandals with her plaid pants, what's the big deal? Soon she will grow out of both and the argument will be moot. Everything in its time.

While looking at this picture, my twenty-year-old looked over my shoulder. "How could you let her go out of the house looking like that?" she snapped. "You would have never let me do that. She looks so silly." Yes, she did, but it didn't seem like argument material this time around. Perhaps it is because at midlife I understood the necessity of being silly at three . . . and wish I was a little sillier at forty-seven.

Resource Guide

References used in addition to information provided to me via the Midlife Motherhood Web site: www.midlifemother.com and at over40babies@yahoo.com

1. The Road Less Traveled

Bureau of Vital Statistics

The U.S. Department of Health and Human Services (see page 245 for further information)

Centers for Disease Control and Prevention (CDC) (see page 245 for further information)

2. In Our Own Words—Common Fears and Concerns

Midlife Mother support group

Creasy and Resnick, eds. *Maternal Fetal Medicine: Practice and Principles*. Philadelphia, PA: W. B. Saunders, 1994.

David S. Newberger, M.D. "Down Syndrome: Prenatal Risk Assessment and Diagnosis." *American Family Physician*. August 15, 2000.

The American Academy of Family Physicians, http://www.aafp.org/afp/20000815/825.html

3. The Challenges of Waiting—Our Race Against Time

William M. Gilbert, M.D., et al. "Childbearing Beyond Age 40: Pregnancy Outcome in 24,032 Cases." *Obstetrics and Gynecology*, Volume 93, January 1999.

"Moms Over 40," Volume 5, Number 1, May–June 1999. UC Davis Health System Publication.

"Injection of Hope." *People*, 10/28/96. Pp. 121–123.

Carla Harkness. *The Infertility Book*. Berkeley, CA: Celestial Arts, 1992.

JoAnne Stone, M.D., et al. *Pregnancy for Dummies*. Foster City, CA: IDG Books, 1999.

Claudia Kalb. "Should You Have Your Baby Now?" *Newsweek*, August 13, 2001. Pp. 40–45.

4. Nine Months and Counting

Stone, et al. *Pregnancy for Dummies*.

Glade B. Curtis, M.D., F.A.C.O.G. *Your Pregnancy After 30*. Tucson, AZ: Fisher Books, 1996.

Katie Tamony. *Your Second Pregnancy*. Chicago: Chicago Review Press, 1995.

Arlene Eisenberg, et al. *What to Expect When You're Expecting (Revised Edition)*. Berkeley, CA: Workingman Publishing Company, 1996.

Dirk Johnson, et al. "Motherhood and Murder." *Newsweek,* July 2, 2001. Pp. 20–25.

5. The Big Event

Stone, et al. *Pregnancy for Dummies*.

Curtis. *Your Pregnancy After 30*.

Tamony. *Your Second Pregnancy*.

6. Finding the New Normal—Getting Adjusted and Dealing with Change

Zachary N. Stowe, M.D., and Charles B. Nemeroff, M.D., Ph.D. *Obstetrics and Gynecology, Women at Risk for Postpartum Depression*. Mosbey-Year Book, 1995.

Harriet Lerner, Ph.D. *The Mother Dance*. New York: HarperCollins, 1998.

Karen Kleinman, M.S.W., and Valerie Raskin, M.D. *This Isn't What I Expected: Overcoming Postpartum Depression*. New York: Bantam Books, 1994.

Postpartum Support International, www.postpartum.net.

7. The Balancing Act—Juggling Work and Motherhood

"Choosing Child Care." *Working Mother Magazine*, February 1995. Pp. 29–33.

Judith Berezin. *The Complete Guide to Choosing Childcare*. The National Association of Child Care Resource and Referral Agencies and Child Care, Inc. New York: Random House, 1990. To order a copy: (800) 677-7760.

Betty Holcomb, et al. "How Does Your State Rate?" *Working Mother Magazine*, July/August, 1999. Pp. 25–40.

Facts on Working Women, U.S. Department of Labor, Women's Bureau, March 2000.

The National Association of Child Care Resource and Referral Agencies. www.naccrra.org

8. Staying "Back in Shape"

Ginny Porter and Jack Holleman. *The Pocket Trainer Strength Training Guide*. El Cerrito, CA: Flexor Press, 2000.

Hope Ricciotti, M.D. and Vincent Connelly. *The Pregnancy Cookbook*. New York: W.W. Norton and Company, 1996.

Christiane Northrup, M.D. *The Wisdom of Menopause*. New York: Bantam, Doubleday, Dell Books, 2001.

Ann Louise Gittleman and Dina Nunziato. *Eat Fat, Lose Weight: How The Right Fats Can Make You Thin for Life*. Lincolnwood, IL: McGraw Hill-NTC, 1999.

Statistical information quoted from:
http://www.protein.com/PTIWeb.nsf/f5ac4132e271703286256735006376aa/21f
e7aed3ea367548625673d0068cf64!OpenDocument#Menopause
Connecticut Team Nutrition Training Program
University of Connecticut, Department of Nutritional Sciences & State Department of Education, Child Nutrition Programs
www.team.uconn.edu

9. Roadside Assistance

Adele Faber and Elaine Mazlish. *Siblings Without Rivalry*. New York: Avon Books, 1987, 1999.

Jann Blackstone-Ford. *The Custody Solutions Sourcebook*. Los Angeles: Lowell House, 1999.

Herbert G. Lingren and Jane Decker. "The Sandwich Generation: A Cluttered Nest." File G1117 under: FAMILY LIFE E-5, Adulthood and Aging. December, 1992. Cooperative Extension, Institute of Agriculture and Natural Resources, University of Nebraska, Lincoln.

Christiane Northrup, M.D. *Women's Bodies, Women's Wisdom*. New York: Bantam Books, 1995 and *The Wisdom of Menopause*.

Bonus Families—a Web site dedicated to the support and reassurance of every member of your stepfamily. www.bonusfamilies.com

Agencies and Literature Supplied By

Ferre Institute Inc.
258 Genesse Street
Suite 302
Utica, NY 13502
(315) 724-4348

The Endometriosis Association
International Headquarters
8585 N. 76th Place
Milwaukee, WI 53223
(414) 355-2200 or (800) 992-3636 in USA, or (800) 426-2362 in Canada

Postpartum Support International
(805) 967-7636
www.postpartum.net
UC Davis Medical Center
Obstetrics and Gynecology
William M. Gilbert, M.D.

Recommended Reading for Adults

Parent School: Simple Lessons from the Leading Experts on Being a Mom or Dad, compiled and edited by Jerry and Lorin Biederman. New York: M. Evans & Company, Inc. 2002.

On Life After Death, Elisabeth Kübler-Ross. Berkeley, CA: Celestial Arts, 1991.

Touchpoints, T. Berry Brazelton, M.D. Boston: Addison-Wesley, 1992.

The Complete Guide to Choosing Child Care, Judith Berezen, copyright 1990, by the National Association of Child Care Resource and Referral Agencies and Child Care, Inc., published by Random House, Inc.

Staying Home: From Full-time Professional to Full-time Parent, Darcie Sanders and Martha M Bullen. Spencer & Waters, rev. 2001.

The Wisdom of Menopause, Christine Northrup, M.D. New York: Bantam, Doubleday, Dell Publishing, 2001.

New Hope for Couples with Infertility Problems, Theresa Foy DiGeronimo. Prima Publishing, 2002.

Great Sex for Moms: Ten Steps to Nurturing Passion While Raising Kids, Valerie Raskin. New York: Fireside, 2002.

Parenting An Only Child: The Joys & Challenges of Raising Your One & Only, Susan Newman, Ph.D. New York: Broadway/Doubleday, 2001.

Expecting Baby: Nine Months of Wonder, Reflection, and Sweet Anticipation, Judy Ford. Berkeley, CA: Conari Press, 2001.

Inconceivable: A Woman's Triumph over Despair and Statistics, Julia Indichova. New York: Broadway Books, 2001.

Mommy or Daddy: Whose Side Am I On? Joel D. Block, Ph.D., and Susan S. Bartell, Psy.D. New York: Adams Media, 2002.

Recommended Reading for Children

I Don't Have an Uncle Phil Anymore, Margorie Pellegrino. Washington, DC: Magination Press, 1999.

This Is How We Became a Family, Wayne Willis. Washington, DC: Magination Press, 2000.

My Parents Are Divorced, Too, Jann Blackstone-Ford. Washington, DC: Magination Press, 1998.

Why Am I An Only Child?, Anuziatta and Nimeroff. Washington, DC: Magination Press, 1998.

Stepliving for Teens, Joel D. Block, Ph.D., and Susan S. Bartell, Psy.D. New York: Price Stern Sloan, 2001.

Web Sites of Interest

www.ivillage.com   Women's Internet community with all kinds of information, including two popular parenting resources:

Parent Soup www.parentsoup.com: Offers expert advice, articles, links, and message boards to women of all ages on parenting toddlers to teens.

Parents Place www.parentsplace.com: Offers information about pregnancy and parenting newborns to toddlers.

www.midlifemother.com   A support site for midlife mothers, featuring departments on common concerns, infertility, juggling work and motherhood, facing menopause and raising toddlers at the same time, nutrition and exercise for women at midlife, plus care for aging parents. Features a message board with links to articles on Parent Soup, www.parentsoup.com, a parenting division of www.ivillage.com.

www.urbandbaby.com   A national Web site to help you find mommy-friendly activities in your area.

www.bonusfamilies.com   Bonus Families is a non-profit organization dedicated to the support and reassurance of every member of your stepfamily. www.bonus families.com is their Web site. It features departments designed specifically for kids of divorce, both biological and bonus parents and grandparents, and Ex-Etiquette, a department that addresses better communication between exes. Offers a message board supported by Parent Soup, a parenting division of www.ivillage.com.

www.hbwm.com   A referral service, and it's linked with other "mom"-friendly sites that can also help you in your search.

www.sohomoms.com   Free job posting and a referral service, and it's linked with other "mom"-friendly sites that can also help you in your search.

www.naccrra.org   The National Association of Child Care Resource and Referral Agencies.

Family.com   Features articles, chats, tips, and more.

www.postpartumstress.com   A support Web site for postpartum depression.

Magazines

Fit Pregnancy (an off-shoot of *Shape* magazine):   A great magazine for pregnant women. Features articles for pregnant midlife mothers on a regular basis. www.fitpregnancy.com

More Magazine: a Meredith Corporation publication, published in the fashion of *Ladies' Home Journal*, caters to women forty and older.

Parenting Magazine: Offers articles, tips, chats on all aspects of pregnancy and raising a child. www.parenting.com

Working Mother Magazine: www.workingmother.com

Reference

Dalkon Shield Claimants Trust
P.O. Box 444
Richmond, VA 23202
(804) 783-8600
Contact for information regarding the claims process for women sustaining injury or infertility from the use of a Dalkon Shield IUD.

Infertility

American Fertility Society
2140 11th Avenue South, Suite 200
Birmingham, AL 35205
(205) 933-8494

RESOLVE, Inc.
1310 Broadway
Somerville, MA 01244
(617) 623-0744
Medical information, emotional support, monthly newsletter, etc. More than 40 local chapters across the United States.
www.resolve.com

PLANNED PARENTHOOD
810 Seventh Avenue
New York, NY 10019
(212) 777-2002

Reproductive Medicine Program
Finch University of Health Sciences
Chicago Medical School
3333 Green Bay Road
North Chicago, IL 60064
(847) 578-3233
Fax: (847) 578-3339
E-mail: info@repro-med.net
Attention: Dr. Alan Beer

Electronic Infertility Network (EIN)
The WIN is an international web-based infertility network whose headquarters is in Carrickfergus, county Antrim.
Postal address: Woodlawn House, Carrickfergus, county Antrium, Northern Ireland, UK
Telephone number: +44 (0)7050 610008
Fax: +44 (0)1960 350450
http://www.ein.org/index.htm
E-mail: webmaster@ein.org

Pregnancy and Birth

Douglas of North America
110 23rd Avenue
Seattle, WA 98112
Fax: (206) 325-0472

Lamaze International
2025 M Street, Suite 800
Washington, DC 20036-3309
(202) 367-1128
Toll-free: (800) 368-4404
Fax: (202) 367-2128

www.lamaze.com offers a range of information about babies and pregnancy on
www.ivillage.com

Bradley American Academy of Husband-Coached Childbirth
Box 5224
Sherman Oaks, CA 91413-5224
1-800-4-A-BIRTH
www.bradleybirth.com

Klinefelter Syndrome

American Association of Klinefelter Syndrome Support (AAKSIS)
Web site that includes up-to-date information on Klinefelter syndrome, complete
with links to other support groups throughout the world.
www.aaksis.com

Klinefelter Association of the UK
http://www.akac70.care4free.net/home.html
National Coordinator
Klinefelter's Syndrome Association
56 Little Yeldham Road
Little Yeldham
Halstead
Essex
CO9 4QT

Turner Syndrome

Turner Syndrome Society of America
Includes information on Turner Syndrome for the U.S. plus international contact
information.
14450 TC Jester, Suite 260
Houston, TX 77014
(832) 249-9988

Toll-free: (800) 365-9944
Fax: (832) 249-9987
http://www.turner-syndrome-us.org/

The U.S. Department of Health and Human Services
200 Independence Avenue, S.W.
Washington, DC 20201
(202) 619-0257
Toll-free: (877) 696-6775

Centers for Disease Control and Prevention (CDC)
Information and statistics on health issues and disease control in the United States.
Public Inquiries/MASO
Mailstop F07
1600 Clifton Road
Atlanta, GA 30333
www.cdc.gov

Aging Parents

Children of Aging Parents
1609 Woodbourne Road
Suite 302-A
Levittown, PA 19057-1511
(215) 945-6900
Toll-free: (800) 227-7294

Family Care Alliance
Toll-free: (800) 445-8106
www.caregiver.org

The National Association for Area Agencies on Aging/Eldercare Locator
Toll-free: (800) 667-1116
www.aoa.dhhs.gov
www.aahsa.org

Adoption

National Committee for Adoption, Inc. (NCFA)
1933 17th Street, N.W.
Washington, DC 20009-6207
(202) 328-1200, hot line: (202) 463-7563

Promotes adoption as a positive family building option. Hot line for referrals and information.

Single Mothers By Choice
P.O. Box 1642
Grace Square Station
New York, NY 10028
(212) 988-0993

North American Council on Adoptable Children (NACAC)
1821 University, Suite N498
St. Paul, MN 55104
(612) 644-3036
Clearinghouse offering general information about children waiting for homes in the United States. Includes special needs adoptions.

Families Adopting Children Everywhere (FACE)
P.O. Box 28058
Baltimore, MD 21239

Adoptive Families of America, Inc.
3333 Highway 100 North
Minneapolis, MN 55422
(612) 535-4829

Childcare

The National Association of Child Care Resources and Referral Agencies (NACCRRA)
1319 F Street, N.W.
Suite 500
Washington, DC 20004
(202) 393-5501
Fax: (202) 393-1109
www.naccrra.org

Child Care Aware
Toll-free: (800) 424-2246
www.childcareaware.org
info@childcareaware.org

Index